Eugene V. Debs home.
Now a registered National Historic Landmark,
in Terre Haute, Indiana

Eugene V. Debs

EUGENE DEBS

American Socialist

by

ANNE TERRY WHITE

LAWRENCE HILL and COMPANY

New York · Westport

Library of Congress Cataloging in Publication Data
White, Anne Terry.
Eugene Debs: American Socialist.
1. Debs, Eugene Victor, 1855–1926—Juvenile literature.
[1. Debs, Eugene Victor, 1855–1926.
2. Labor and laboring classes—Biography]
I. Title.
HX84.D3W48 335'.3'0924 [B] [92] 74-9350
ISBN 0-88208-045-8

Photo credits

1. Klein & Guttenstein. Eugene V. Debs Foundation.
2. Richard H. Bruce. Eugene V. Debs Foundation.
3. Richard Penton. Collection of Stanley King.
4. Richard Penton. Collection of Stanley King.
5. Eugene V. Debs Foundation.
6. Richard Penton. Collection of Stanley King.
7. Eugene V. Debs Foundation.
8. Eugene V. Debs Foundation.
9 and 10. Richard Penton. Collection of Stanley King.
11. Eugene V. Debs Foundation.

Copyright © 1974 Anne Terry White
ISBN 0-88208-045-8
Library of Congress Catalog card number: LC 74-9350
First edition October 1974
Lawrence Hill & Co., Inc.
Manufactured in the United States of America
by Ray Freiman & Company

Contents

To
Susan

EUGENE DEBS

American Socialist

1

A Boy in Terre Haute

Frontier Terre Haute had a lively air of ''get ahead'' about it in the 1850s. Nearly 6,000 people lived in the Indiana town. Wages were low. But if a man got his hands on ten dollars, he tried to make it twenty. There were hogs to slaughter, pork to ship on flatboats to New Orleans. Money! Get it!

Eugene Debs did not sense the drive—he was too young. And his parents, selling meat and groceries in the front room of their two-story frame house, were not caught up in it. All they wanted was to make a living for their growing family. Watching the careful pennies swept into the cashbox, they were amused to note what small interest their boy took in the trade. Eugene needed no urging to keep from underfoot.

Paper boats could be sailed in the puddles that splotched the clay roads after a rain. Half a block from his home ran a broad canal. There were boats to watch for, sticks to throw in. Eugene was fascinated by the sluggish water, always going, going, carrying his sticks with it. But most of all he loved the railroad, two blocks away.

Eugene remembered the first time his father took him to watch the freight go clattering and rumbling by, black smoke streaming from its stack. Through the cab window he had seen a man in a blue coat and cap with a visor. He looked proud. His eyes were fixed on the tracks ahead.

"That's the engineer," his father had said. "He makes the train go."

A red-faced fireman had just thrown a chunk of wood into the firebox of the locomotive. He waved back . . . .

When the Civil War broke out, Eugene was five, having been born on the fifth of November, 1855. He didn't quite know what the war meant except that there was fighting and glory, which was something exciting, like fireworks. Most of Terre Haute was for the Union and sided with the North against the South. The South didn't want union. What the South wanted was to be a separate country and have black people for slaves. That's what Eugene's father told him.

There were black people in Terre Haute—not many. Eugene stared at them curiously. His father said that young black men wanted to fight so that all black people in the country could be free. He said that people all over the world had fought for freedom. His father knew. He read big books.

What was freedom?

4

A Boy in Terre Haute

These days Eugene didn't sail boats so much. He watched men drill, watched troop trains moving out on the tracks. The locomotive and string of cars had a new meaning now. The cars were carrying soldiers. Where to? Where was the engineer taking these big boys and men with muskets? To glory?

What was glory?

Eugene felt somehow that his father was different from other men in Terre Haute. His voice was gentle, and he spoke German as well as French. He had come from the other side of the ocean, from Alsace, where people spoke those languages instead of English, and where he had bitterly quarreled with his father, a rich man who owned textile mills. The quarrel was about marrying Marguerite, Eugene's mother, whom everybody called Daisy. The rich father didn't want his son Daniel to marry a simple working girl in a mill. ''It will ruin your career,'' the father had said. Daniel said that whom he married was his own business. Then his father suddenly died, and Daniel came to America to make his way. Marguerite had not wanted Daniel to ''sacrifice his career'' for her, but when he threatened to kill himself, she joined him in New York.

Eugene never tired of hearing how job followed job, how a little girl was born and died, how another came. The family had finally settled in Terre Haute because so many French people from Canada lived in the town. Eugene's mother had taken their last $40, invested it in groceries, and opened a store in their front room. Daniel knew how to butcher. The French people liked Daniel and Daisy Debs and traded in their store. So there was a living for the family. . . .

Eugene started school. He didn't like it—school was the same

5

thing over and over, he said. He liked better to learn what his father taught him on Sunday. Eugene learned to speak French and German. He went with his father on long tramps and learned the names of different birds and flowers. Sometimes they took the dogs and a gun along and hunted snipe and prairie chickens. Many a Sunday they brought home a treasure of mushrooms, over which Eugene's mother clapped her hands. She made a big fuss about mushrooms. Up near the ceiling of their kitchen, strings of mushrooms hung drying.

Sundays after dinner Daniel read aloud from his books while Eugene listened. "To be a great writer is to be a great man," Daniel said. The busts Eugene saw high on the book shelves were of Daniel's favorite authors. All these men believed in freedom. They had written things that had inspired people and made them want to fight for a better life. That was what freedom meant—a better life.

Why did they have to *fight* for it? Eugene wondered. Why didn't they just *have* it?

There was one book which, when Eugene was old enough, he read over and over again. That was Victor Hugo's *Les Miserables*. His own middle name was Victor. His father had loved Victor Hugo's books so much that he wanted his son to have part of the writer's name. *Les Miserables* absorbed Eugene. It opened for him a question with which he would be concerned all his life: *What was justice?*

The hero of the book was a man who had suffered great misfortune. As an unemployed laborer, he had stolen a loaf of bread to feed his sister's starving orphan children. He had been caught in the act and sent to prison. In that hell he had spent

6

A Boy in Terre Haute

nineteen years. Cruelty, hardship, indifference had changed Jean Valjean from a man into a brute. The mercy of a bishop had changed him back into a man.

Why did prisons have to be so cruel?

Eugene thought about that. He thought about justice and about freedom that meant a better life for everybody.

Eugene loved to turn over ideas in his mind, but he did not like to study. When he was fourteen, he entered high school. It made him feel as if he were tied up. The working world called to him and he wanted to break loose. There were six children in the family now. Why shouldn't he help feed them?

At fourteen Eugene was six feet tall, lean, strong—and stubborn. His parents didn't want their boy to drop out of school. But Eugene argued till Daniel and Daisy were forced to let him have his way. Daniel himself helped Eugene find a job. Terre Haute had grown, had become a railroad center, and Daniel had a friend who worked in the paint shop of the Vandalia Railroad. Could he help Eugene?

Eugene got a job in the paint shop. It was dull work, even for one who was in love with trains. He had to scrape off the grease that splashed from the wheels and hardened on the bottom of freight cars. The potash Eugene used to loosen the grease made his fingers crack and bleed. The work was tiring, monotonous, the hours seemed endless. He was just a boy, down on the bottom, ordered about and sworn at by everybody. What comfort was it to know that those who swore at him were sworn at in turn by those above them?

Eugene earned fifty cents a day. But when on Saturday night he handed his three dollars to his mother and saw the pride in her

7

eyes, he knew he would have the strength to go back on Monday.

Doggedly he stuck to his job. It was a welcome promotion when he was sent with a crew to paint all the switches on the track as far as Indianapolis, seventy-five miles away. After that he was set to painting stripes on car bodies. From there it was just a step to doing lettering on locomotives.

Eugene had been working on the railroad over a year when one evening as he was painting stripes on a car, an engineer burst into the shop. His "damfool" fireman had got drunk and hadn't shown up for work! Someone had to shovel coal for him! The engineer's eyes fell on Eugene.

"How about him?" the engineer barked.

The boss of the paint shop nodded O.K.

Eugene became a locomotive fireman at a dollar a night.

2

Eugene Joins a Brotherhood

As soon as his wages went up a little more, Eugene registered at a business school. He slept a few hours in the morning, went to school in the afternoon, and fired the locomotive at night. Now he was sorry he had quit school. It was a bitter day for him when his high school class graduated without him.

But a worse blow was in store. The Vandalia Railroad shut down, and Eugene lost his job.

He wasn't the only one. He didn't understand how "hard times" had come about, but something that would later be called a depression had overtaken the country. Terre Haute no longer wore its lively air of "get ahead." Unemployed men shuffled along the sidewalks and huddled together on street corners.

Eugene hopped a freight. Maybe in some other town there

would be work. In St. Louis he found a job as a locomotive fireman.

Now Eugene saw sights he had never witnessed before. Things were bad enough in Terre Haute, but here he saw scenes that reminded him of *Les Miserables*. He saw families dispossessed, saw women and children sitting on piled-up furniture on the sidewalk. Tarpaper shacks sprang up on the Mississippi mudflats. Starving children ate mud.

Throughout it all Eugene kept at his job of firing. When he wasn't working, he buried himself in a book. He read anything, everything. And meantime his mother worried about her boy. She had good reason. To cut costs, railroads were using worn-out rails, rickety trestles, couplings that broke at a jolt. Every day workers were crushed between cars. Railroad accidents were so frequent that the newspapers didn't bother to report them unless a lot of people were hurt. Sometimes Eugene would find himself standing with his companions beside a broken engine. Often he helped to carry a bruised and bleeding body back to a wife and child. A friend of Eugene's slipped and was killed under a locomotive. When Daisy heard about that, she begged Eugene to come home. Eugene idolized his mother. He threw up his job and left for Terre Haute.

Back home, he took the only job that was offered. His father dealt with a wholesale grocer who was also his good friend. Herman Hulman hired Eugene as a billing clerk to keep track of the boxes, bags, and bales that moved in and out of his warehouse. Eugene counted and marked, counted and marked. Then he wrote the numbers down in a ledger. He hated everything about his job except the pay, but he stuck it out with Hulman & Cox for five

10

Eugene Joins a Brotherhood

years. With part of his first wages he bought himself an encyclopedia—one way or another he was going to get an education.

The railroad kept calling to him. Evenings he would go down to the tracks and watch the engines back and switch. He envied the men who were fixing broken couplings. Well he knew the hardships of the rail in snow and sleet and hail, yet he envied the locomotive firemen.

One evening in 1875 he heard by chance that the Grand Master of the Brotherhood of Locomotive Firemen was coming to Terre Haute to organize a union. Eugene went to the meeting. He wanted so much to belong to the Brotherhood! He had read how in the French Revolution people had shouted: "Liberty! Equality! Brotherhood!" The word *brotherhood* had deep meaning for him.

"I'm not working as a locomotive fireman right now," he said to the Grand Master. "But couldn't I join the Brotherhood just the same?"

The Grand Master looked at the lanky nineteen-year-old boy. So few men had signed up that there was no sense in being too fussy. "My boy," he said, gently putting his large, rough hand on Eugene's shoulder and looking deep into his eyes, "you're a little young. But I believe you're in earnest and will make your mark in the Brotherhood."

"I'll do my best," Eugene assured him.

The blood was fairly leaping in his veins. Brotherhood! He belonged to a Brotherhood. It was like—like—"As if someone had his arm around you," Eugene thought.

How uplifted he felt to be made at once secretary of Vigo Lodge No. 16! He went to every meeting. He took careful notes.

The thing that interested him most was that the Brotherhood was in part an insurance scheme. He knew well that locomotive firemen were often injured or killed and that their wives and children were left in want. He was glad to see the brothers protected. But the brothers weren't interested in insurance. What they wanted was a union that would raise their wages, shorten their hours, and stand up to the bosses. One by one the members dropped out. Sometimes the secretary would go to a Vigo lodge meeting and find that nobody else showed up. He sat alone till closing time, then picked up his notebook and went home. For ten years he never missed a meeting.

1877 was a crisis year in America. The Pennsylvania Railroad and the Baltimore and Ohio posted notices that there would be wage cuts. The railroad workers read the notices with rising rage, tore them down, and spat upon them. They weren't going to work for less money! No, Sir! Engineers and locomotive firemen stepped down from their cabs and walked off. They blocked the rails so that nobody else could run the trains.

The local militia was sent out to deal with the strikers. It would not fire on them. But when strikers in West Virginia and Maryland burned hundreds of locomotives and freight cars, President Hayes sent out federal troops. These didn't hesitate to shoot, nor did the soldiers imported from Philadelphia to crush the strikers in Pittsburgh. More than a hundred workers were killed and hundreds were wounded. Inside of two weeks the strikers were begging to have their jobs back.

But the employers had the workers at their mercy now and wouldn't take back anyone who had been active in the walkout.

Eugene Joins a Brotherhood

When a man did get rehired, he had to sign a "yellow dog" contract, promising not to join a union.

Although the Brotherhood of Locomotive Firemen had stayed out of the bloody events, twenty-two-year-old Eugene—
—still working for Hulman & Cox—was shaken. *The Locomotive Firemen's Magazine* insisted that the walkout was the fault of the railroads. It said that the workers were so oppressed that they *had* to walk off their jobs. But he was upset by the violence—the workers' violence—and his thoughts were different. What had brotherhood to do with violence? Were they going to destroy *order*? Were the railroad workers to pay no attention to the *laws* of the land? Would they stain their hands with the crimson blood of their fellow human beings?

"No! a thousand times No!" Eugene declared. It was 1878 and he was speaking at the national convention of the Brotherhood of Locomotive Firemen in Buffalo. Instead of walking off their jobs, the railroad workers should have talked things over with the bosses. If they had, they would have made the employers see their point of view. Employers were reasonable men, they wanted to play fair. Eugene was positive that disputes between employers and employees could be settled by talking things over. Compromise—that was the way. Each side had to give in a little.

The locomotive firemen listened to Debs and sensed how sure of himself he was. "He's a spellbinder," they said admiringly. They weren't at all sure they agreed with him; nevertheless they chose him to be associate editor of *The Magazine*.

Not long after this the Brotherhood unexpectedly turned to Eugene again. The BLF was in deep trouble: their secretary-

13

treasurer had disappeared, nobody knew where, and had left the Brotherhood six thousand dollars in debt. Nobody but Debs, the grand master said, could save the Brotherhood.

Eugene panicked. He didn't want to be secretary-treasurer. The responsibility under the circumstances was too great. Over and over again he said he couldn't—then under pressure said he would. What else could he do when the Brotherhood needed him so badly?

In 1879 Eugene had left Hulman & Cox because he had been elected city clerk of Terre Haute. He didn't as yet know that he would be city clerk for four years. But now there was this big, new responsibility. He had to bring back to life a dying organization——in his spare time. The BLF moved its national office to Terre Haute, and Debs took over. Out of his own savings he paid $1,000 to cover the outstanding insurance claims. He gave his own note to hold off the printer. He got all the officers and employees of the BLF to take no salary for the time being. In 1882 he gave half his salary as city clerk to the BLF while taking no salary at all from the Brotherhood.

Day after day Eugene put in sixteen and eighteen hours. Sometimes dawn would find him writing an editorial for *The Magazine* or answering a letter of inquiry. Sometimes he fell asleep over his writing. His mother's hand would turn out the light, and he would go to bed protesting. Many a night, often on Sundays, and every time he had a couple of days off, Eugene was on the road. His grip was always packed. He rode on engines over mountain and plain, slept on the floor of cabooses, was fed from the lunchpails of locomotive firemen. Many a time he tramped in rain and snow half the night to organize a new lodge or bring to life

14

Eugene Joins a Brotherhood

one that existed only on paper. He was put off trains for riding without a ticket, ordered out of roundhouses for being an "agitator." But he added lodge to lodge. By 1881 the membership had doubled. The next year it went up to 5,000. By 1883 he had got the Brotherhood out of the red.

Something that happened about this time convinced the members that Eugene could be trusted to stand up for their interests:

An unimportant official of the Brotherhood of Locomotive Firemen came to Eugene with a complaint. He said he had been thrown out of the office of a vice-president of the Pennsylvania Railroad.

Eugene grabbed his hat. The two union men caught the first freight for Columbus and were shown into the office of the vice-president of the Pennsylvania. Eugene was quietly beginning to explain their errand when the vice-president cut him short.

"Before we go any further," he said in a loud voice, "I want you to know, Debs, that I don't give a God damn for the BLF."

"And I want you to know," Eugene returned in a voice equally loud, "that I don't give a God damn for the Pennsylvania Railroad. I'm not here to get your opinion of us. I'm here to get courteous treatment for our officials!"

The conversation lasted an hour. It ended with the vice-president offering Eugene a job with the company.

"No, thanks," Eugene replied. "I like what I'm doing."

The vice-president was taken aback. "At least you'll accept an annual pass on the Pennsylvania," he said.

"No, thanks," Eugene said firmly. He didn't want to be beholden to the company for anything.

All across the Great Plains the story of what happened was proudly repeated by railroad workers. Eugene Debs had stood up to the vice-president of the Pennsylvania Railroad, and the Railroad had given in!

3

"Justice" in Chicago

Debs was popular not only in the BLF. In all Terre Haute there wasn't a man better liked. Everybody—poor and rich—was Eugene's friend. Everyone knew him to be honest, hard-working, brave, devoted, intelligent, sincere, friendly—and a man who loved a good joke. "Gene" everybody called him. That in itself meant something. He had the warm affection of the whole town.

He was always doing something for somebody. If a person came to him with a problem, he immediately made the problem his own. He was more than generous with money; he was positively reckless with it. His pocket was open to anyone who asked and many who did not.

"He'd give you the shirt off his back," people said of Debs. They respected and admired him. He was everything that midwesterners liked—one of the boys, and yet head and shoulders above them. He was a man whom workers could follow.

His parents adored him—and he them. His young brother Theodore, who had become bookkeeper for the BLF at $10 a week, worshiped Eugene. Two of Eugene's sisters were helping out in the office. And now there was Kate Metzel—it looked as if Eugene would ask her to marry him. But these people were just the inner circle. The outer circle was vastly wider.

Traveling around, organizing BLF lodges, Eugene got close to all sorts of railroad workers. He talked to switchmen, brakemen, section hands, conductors, telegraphers, engineers. He helped the brakemen form a union. He was ready to help any workers who wanted to organize. It was for their protection, he said. For on all sides, Eugene heard complaints. The wages were low, the jobs unsteady, the bosses arrogant. Workers told him they were tired of being blacklisted and barred from jobs, tired of yellow-dog contracts, of long hours, of having to knuckle under. They didn't want to strike, but if they had to, by God they would.

Debs told everybody that he believed in arbitration. Employers were men of good will. If workers would only talk things over with them, there would be no need to strike.

The men shrugged their shoulders in doubt. They'd like to see some of that precious good will Debs talked about!

At their 1885 convention, the Brotherhood of Locomotive Firemen got rid of all their officers who didn't approve of strikes. Debs tried to resign. The delegates wouldn't let him—they liked him too well, they owed him too much, they couldn't get along

18

"Justice" in Chicago

without Debs. Let him go on believing in arbitration if that's the way he saw it. They wanted him to keep on as secretary-treasurer of the BLF and editor of *The Magazine.*

Debs stayed on.

As editor, occasionally he made mistakes in judgment, but they were mostly minor ones. Under his editorship, *The Magazine's* circulation grew as never before, for Debs threw himself into his writing with passion. Often he would get up in the middle of the night to develop some idea that struck him. And the article or editorial shaped itself convincingly. Debs seemed to have his finger on his readers' pulse, knew just what to say, just what the railroad workers were ready for, just what they wanted to hear. It was because he had come up from the ranks. He understood his readers. To be sure, he was a conservative—the favorite of the railroad corporations. They approved of him when he said that the BLF was not engaged in any quarrel between capital and labor. They applauded when he said that there could be no quarrel unless it was caused by ''deliberate piracy on one side and unreasonable demands on the other.'' They did not resent it even when Debs said, ''All that labor wants is a fair day's pay for a fair day's work.''

In 1886 a campaign for the eight-hour day was being waged throughout the country. Chicago, where anarchists were prominent in the struggle, was the very heart of the eight-hour movement. On the first of May, 40,000 Chicago workers laid down their tools. It was well known that the employers stood solidly against the eight-hour day and the city was tense. What would happen?

19

It didn't take long. On the third of May, police killed a striker at the McCormick reaper works. Outraged by the murder, the anarchists called a protest meeting. It was to take place the following evening at Haymarket Square.

Due to a steady rain, the meeting was not very large. It was also very quiet. By ten o'clock a good many people had already gone home. It was then that a police captain, a man much hated in Chicago because he was so brutal, led in 180 of his men to scatter what was left of the crowd. As the police approached the speakers' wagon, a bomb was thrown. It seemed to have come from the sidewalk. The bomb killed a policeman and wounded 65 others of the patrol, six of them fatally. The police started firing into the crowd killing several and wounding some 200.

Labor leaders and workers of the rank and file in various parts of the city were quickly arrested. Finally, eight anarchists—all union men—were indicted for the murder of one of the policemen.

Six of the indicted men had not even been at the meeting. The other two clearly had nothing to do with throwing the bomb. But several had been leaders in the eight-hour movement, and the judge knew what the employers wanted. He claimed that if the accused had ever said anything that might incite others to violence, they were just as guilty of the crime as if they had committed it themselves. They didn't even need to be on the spot when the crime took place. This was contrary to American law. Yet the judge instructed the jury to make up their minds on that basis.

The eight anarchists were convicted of murder.

Newspapers did their best to prejudice people against the condemned. But there was also a great outcry against the judg-

"Justice" in Chicago

ment. Frame-up! Unfair! Improper! The judge was prejudiced! Even United States senators and bankers said it.

Eugene did not add his voice to the outcry. He had no sympathy for anarchist ideas, and he did not believe in violence. Yet free speech was a burning issue with him, and he passionately believed that the anarchists were framed. Doubtless he thought that he had no right to voice his personal views as long as he was editor of *The Magazine*—to do so would be to bring unfavorable attention to the Brotherhood. He would betray his readers. For five months he struggled with himself and remained silent. When he did speak, it was already too late. By that time nothing and no one could save the anarchists.

Four of the condemned men were hanged. Three were sent to prison. One killed himself in jail. He was twenty-one years old.

Eugene never forgot the victims, nor the words spoken by one of the condemned on the scaffold, when the nooses had already been adjusted and the caps pulled down: "There will come a time when our silence will be more powerful than the voices you are strangling today."

Twenty-five thousand people marched in the funeral procession. "I loved these men!" their defense counsel said over the graves.

Eugene loved them, too. Time and again he wrote about them. He talked about them in his speeches. Many times he went to visit the cemetery where the men were buried. It seems clear that the martyrs weighed heavily on his mind.

4

A Union to Include All

Eugene learned as he went along, learned from events, from people, from books.

One from whom he learned much was Samuel Gompers, chief of the New York cigarmakers. Debs respected Gompers's fierce belief in the rights of labor and admired the American Federation of Labor into which Gompers had organized various trade unions of skilled workers. Thoughts of federation flitted through his own mind. If the railway brotherhoods were federated and stood shoulder to shoulder, he thought, they could win their strikes.

For by now, having had a closer look at employers, Eugene had changed his mind about strikes. By the late 1880s he had come to feel that the strike was the best weapon workers had, and he didn't hesitate to say so in *The Magazine*. Anyone who didn't believe in strikes didn't know his history, he said. What had reduced the workday from fourteen hours? Strikes. What had raised wages? Strikes. A fair day's pay was not going to drop like a ripe apple into the workers' lap. It was something that had to be won by struggle.

The brotherhoods were looking to Debs to lead them. "Now is the time," he said, and he made a strong effort to federate the railway unions.

But federation didn't work. Instead of standing shoulder to shoulder, each brotherhood selfishly did what was good for itself. Debs was so outraged by the show of selfishness that he made up his mind to quit as BLF secretary-treasurer. He wanted to give up being editor of *The Magazine,* too, but, under great pressure, yielded on this point.

It was hard to accept failure. Eugene's dream of united action, however, was too powerful to be shattered, for he had not lost his faith in workers. Hadn't he seen poor families in St. Louis sharing the little food they had with families that had none? Railway men would stick together if only he could find the right cement.

He understood why federation had failed: the brotherhoods were built on crafts and for that reason tended to separate. He had to build a different kind of organization, one in which the groups were not pitted against one another. It must be a union that included *all* railroad workers, lowly trackers who earned a dollar or less a day as well as the higher paid engineers. Perhaps there were as many as 700,000 railroad men who had never been

A Union to Include All

organized. He was convinced that if all were organized in all branches of the service, and all acted together, they could win their rights.

Debs was confident because he did not yet appreciate how strong the corporations were. Only vaguely did he sense that they were set on wiping out all the workers' organizations. He didn't wake up until after the steel strike at Homestead, Pennsylvania, left the strongest union in America in pieces. He didn't realize what was ahead for labor till the miners at Coeur d'Alene, Idaho, were forced to fight a pitched battle with strikebreakers, and President Harrison sent in the Army to smash the strike.

"Watch out!" Debs warned in *The Magazine*. "Let 1892 be a lesson to unions."

He worked day and night to complete his plan. Kate, who had become his wife in 1885, did all she could to lessen the sense of pressure, but he felt it nevertheless. For just then the country had slid into a depression. Banks were closing and people were losing the savings of a lifetime. Factories shut down. Once again jobless men, hands deep in empty pockets, huddled on street corners. Women dug for scraps in garbage cans.

There were so many angles to work out! Because his union would include all railroad workers, he was counting on an enormous membership. For this reason he felt he could afford to make the dues very low, so low that the humblest railroad worker could pay them. He reasoned that many men paying small dues would build up the union treasury just as well as a few men paying high dues. It was to be a truly national union. He would call it the American Railway Union.

On June 20, 1893, Debs was ready to disclose his plan.

Fifty leaders of railway labor met that day in Chicago to talk things over. They were dismayed by what the depression was doing to railroad workers and wanted to do something about it. Debs told them what he had in mind. Some already knew—Debs had been in touch with them—but there was so much that was new and strange in the idea of one big union where everybody was equal. Strangest of all was that the president of the union was to be no better paid than the rank and file. They couldn't get over the idea that Debs had set his own salary at a mere seventy-five dollars a month.

"I do this," Eugene explained, "because it pleases me. I have a heart for others, and that is why I am in this work. I do not consider that I have made any sacrifices whatever; no man does unless he violates his conscience. If I rise," he ended, "it will be *with* the ranks, not *from* them."

By evening the fifty railroaders were won over, and next day the newspapers carried a full account of the plan. Any "white" worker who served a railroad in any way at all could belong to the American Railway Union. Engineers and conductors, engine wipers and men working on the roadbed, even coal miners and longshoremen if they served a railroad could belong. All of them would be equal in the union.

Debs didn't like the fact that only "white" workers could join the union. He was no racist. Nor were quite a few of the men at the meeting that day. They argued long and hard to have the union open to blacks. Eugene and those on his side finally gave in—they knew there was heavy prejudice inside the brotherhoods, and they wanted the American Railway Union to become a fact.

The news was sensational. But six days later another sensa-

26

A Union to Include All

tion displaced the ARU in the press. This news was so unexpected, so much desired by Debs, that even he stopped thinking about the union. John Peter Altgeld, who had recently become governor of Illinois, had pardoned the three remaining Haymarket anarchists!

In 1886 there had been a great outcry when the eight anarchists were sentenced. Now there was an even greater outcry—from the other side. If the governor had pardoned the prisoners as an act of mercy, probably very few people would have protested. But this was not an act of mercy. Altgeld had studied the records of the case for months and had concluded that a great injustice had been done. It was late, but he was going to do what he could to set things right. He couldn't bring the dead to life, but he could pardon three living men who were not guilty. They had been in prison for seven years.

Altgeld knew that to pardon these men was an unpopular thing to do. He knew he was risking his career by letting the anarchists out. But he could not live with his conscience if he failed to do it.

Neither could Eugene Debs live with *his* conscience if he failed to stand by the governor. Debs now wrote in *The Magazine* what he had wanted to write seven years ago. And he got the same treatment that Governor Altgeld got. Spite and rage and prejudice poured out on Eugene. He let them roll over him. He had been a stubborn boy. He was a stubborn man.

When he picked up the ARU where he had left it, Debs had a much lighter heart. He had taken it for granted that the engineers wouldn't like the idea of having pick-and-shovel men be their equals in the union. He didn't care. He saw the brotherhoods with their high dues shrink and shrink while the ARU grew and grew. The union was growing so fast that the organizers couldn't keep up

27

with the applications. Unskilled workers rushed into the ARU, rushed in joyously, confidently. They had been left out, unprotected, underpaid, driven. Now these unskilled workers would have a chance to stand together with skilled men for the rights of all. And it would cost them so little! Never had there been such a spirit among railroad workers. In a single year the ARU built 465 lodges. In twelve months it had enrolled 150,000 members. The knowledge that Eugene Debs had given up a salary of $4,000 a year to take only $75 a month as president of the ARU won many to his side. Here was a *real* leader! Here was a man they wanted to follow—a man who wished to rise *with* the ranks, not *from* the ranks.

But the railroads were not intimidated by the new union. The depression was on their side. With three million jobless in the country, the railroads felt they could cut wages and get away with it.

In August 1893, James J. Hill, one of the most powerful men in America and owner of the Great Northern Railroad, reduced wages. He cut them again in January 1894. In March came a third cut. By this time even his engineers were getting only eighty dollars a month. Unskilled workers were getting less than forty, and some were trying to support their families on a dollar a day. Hill received a letter from the ARU. It told him that his employees would strike unless he raised wages. The owner of the Great Northern didn't even bother to reply.

A strike was called. It spread all across the Northwest.

"Fire anybody who is known to be sympathetic to the union!" Hill told his superintendents.

Big signs were posted by the company. Any interference with

28

A Union to Include All

the mails would be punished by a fine of $10,000 and two years in prison.

But nobody even tried to stop the mails. Debs had said, "Let the trains carrying mail go through!" And they did. They were the only trains that moved in all the Northwest.

James Hill tried every trick he knew. Each time Debs saw through it and came out on top. The labor leader knew that he was in a strong position. For the new cement was holding. The 9,000 strikers on the Great Northern were standing shoulder to shoulder. Eighteen days after the Great Northern strike began, Hill settled through arbitration. The strikers won 97½ percent of their demands.

James Hill himself unbent and joked with Debs about it. But the strain of those eighteen days had been terrific, and Debs wanted no celebration—he wanted to get home.

As the train that was taking him to Terre Haute moved slowly out of the yards of St. Paul, Minnesota, Eugene stood on the rear platform. On either side of the train, leaning on their shovels and lifting their hats, stood a crowd of old trackers. Debs's eyes filled with tears as he waved his hat to them. He had never felt so highly honored. These men, whose bodies were bent with weary toil for which they received from eighty cents to a dollar a day, were giving him the only thing they could—their esteem. They were thanking him for leading them to victory.

5

Driven as Far as They Would Go

George Pullman was a cabinet maker in his youth. One time he had occasion to pass the night on a train. He had found the sleeping car very uncomfortable. Why, he asked himself, was sleeping on a train so much worse than sleeping on a steamboat? He worked on the idea. He hinged two seat cushions together to form a lower berth. In the wall above, he devised a way of hiding an upper berth. Pullman's sleeping car had the advantage of turning into a day coach in the daytime.

The railroads weren't much interested in the invention at first because, to use it, coaches had to be higher and wider. But when people started traveling all the way across the continent by train, comfortable sleeping cars became a must. Pretty soon railways were raising bridges and moving station platforms to suit Pullman's palace cars. George Pullman made a fortune.

He forgot that he had once been a workingman. Now he belonged to the moneyed class, and his sympathies were with the rich. The workers in his shops became for him not human beings like himself but so many hands.

After setting up his Palace Car Company in various places, he built a plant in a suburb south of Chicago. He called the company town *Pullman*. He liked having a town called by his name. He liked being absolute ruler there as well as in the plant. George Pullman owned all the houses, all the schools, the churches, the theater, the library. His town was supposed to be a model community. Yet the rents were actually 20 to 25 percent higher than for the same kind of dwellings in nearby suburbs. And the charges for water and gas were higher. Pullman bought water and gas in Chicago and resold them at a profit. He made money out of everything. People even had to pay for borrowing books from the library.

When Pullman cut wages in the factory, the rents stayed the same. "There's no connection," George Pullman said. "Rents are one thing, wages another."

There was deep discontent in Pullman. The workers felt as if they, too, were owned by Pullman. They couldn't get along on what they earned, yet they kept on living in the town. They said they stayed because the workers who lived in Pullman were the last to be laid off and the first to be taken on.

1893 was a depression year. George Pullman was making enormous profits, but just the same between 1893 and 1894 he cut wages 25 to 50 per cent.

Driven as Far as They Would Go

In the winter of 1894 the suffering in Pullman became unbearable. To keep warm in houses that had no coal, children had to stay in bed all day. Bitter thoughts filled the minds of those who had been laid off. No work, no money, no credit at the store.

Spring came. Men who were still employed felt desperate about their wage cuts. After their rent was deducted, most had no more than one to six dollars to live on for two weeks. Who could support a family on that? If only they could strike a blow at Pullman! But how? Some 4,000 workers joined the American Railway Union. They could do that because Pullman owned a short track near the factory.

A workers' committee finally went to see the company's vice-president, Wickes.

"Put your complaint in writing," Wickes told them.

Pullman himself came to the next meeting. He said that he wasn't selling as many cars as he had been. The plant was working at a loss, and he was keeping the shops open just to furnish work for the men. His business didn't warrant any increase in wages. He did not mention that besides paying its stockholders 8 percent a year, the company had a surplus of over two million dollars. This was more than the entire wage bill for six months.

An official of the ARU was on the watch. He sent Debs a wire: There might be a walkout at Pullman.

Debs himself didn't know what the situation in Pullman was. He advised caution. But the workers were too desperate to be stopped by anyone. They struck. They didn't know how their strike would come out. They didn't have much hope. All they knew was that they had been driven as far as they could go. Three thousand workers walked out of the Pullman shops. Three hundred

33

remained. That evening the company posted a notice on the entrance gate of the plant: *These works are closed until further notice*.

In the middle of May, Debs went to Pullman. The ARU had not called the strike, but the strikers were members of the union, and it was Debs's business to find out if they had just cause to strike.

Arriving in the company town, he was surrounded by the workers. Debs heard shocking things. A skilled mechanic told him that he had worked for twelve days and been paid seven cents. Actually his wages had been $9.07, but $9.00 had been taken off in advance for rent. Another worker said he had only *four* cents left after his rent had been deducted.

But high rents and low wages were not all that the men resented. They were constantly sworn at and insulted by their superiors and were laid off for the least offense, never to be rehired. It made no difference how long the man had worked for the company. Compensation? Try and get it! Unless compelled to, the company would pay nothing to a man who got hurt while working. The company doctor made out the report, and he was always on the company's side. Nor would Pullman willingly grant anything to the family of a worker who was killed on the job. Pensions were unknown. Many an injured or retired worker was living out his last days in the poorhouse.

Debs walked through Pullman on his own, looking at the houses, talking to the women and children. He had come to see for himself, and the picture he got stood out starkly in black and white. On one side he saw greed, on the other side, misery. George Pullman was a robber! The workers were striking to prevent

Driven as Far as They Would Go

Pullman from turning them into slaves! Before he left, Debs told the workers to send a committee to Chicago, where on June 12 the first convention of the ARU was going to be held. "Tell your story to the delegates," he said. "Let them hear from your lips why Pullman workers went on strike."

It was some days before the convention got around to hearing the committee. But many of the 425 delegates had already been to Pullman and seen for themselves the terrible conditions there. They listened with sympathy when the committee read its statement:

"We struck because we were without hope. We joined the American Railway Union because it gave us a glimmer of hope. We will make you proud of us, brothers, if you will give us the hand we need."

Indignant voices were heard:

"George Pullman has gone too far!"

"It's time we showed that bloodsucker!"

"The ARU shouldn't let a single sleeping car move till Pullman settles with the workers!"

Debs restrained the delegates. He didn't want them to take hasty action. This was no time to strike when unemployed men stood on every street corner, just waiting for a chance to get a job. The brotherhoods were unfriendly. Some of them might even provide strikebreakers. Most important, the ARU wasn't ready to take on Pullman. A strike against Pullman was bound to be a long-drawn-out affair, and the ARU had just been through a strike and had no strike funds. Let a committee of twelve men, including six strikers, call on the company and propose arbitration.

A committee was quickly chosen. But it might as well not

35

have gone—the company would have nothing to do with representatives of the American Railway Union.

When the committee came back and reported, the delegates
were furious. They were ready for *any* action now.

Again Debs restrained them. Let another committee, he said,
made up of Pullman employees only, go to the company and ask
for arbitration.

The committee returned empty-handed. Vice-president
Wickes had flatly told them there was nothing to arbitrate.

ARU delegates wired to their local unions for instructions.
"Use your judgment," the locals wired back.

So a committee was chosen to recommend what should be
done. Debs pleaded to give Pullman another chance. "Let no
move be made without one last conference with the company!" he
said.

All right—four days more. If in that time the company didn't
agree to arbitrate, then the Pullman shops at Ludlow, Kentucky,
and at St. Louis should be struck. Furthermore, there should be a
boycott; all ARU men should refuse to handle Pullman cars.

Again Wickes would not settle the dispute peacefully.

There was no alternative. The delegates voted to support the
walkout, the boycott to begin at noon on June 26—unless the
Pullman Company changed its mind.

6

The Biggest Strike in America

Pullman had no intention of settling. He stubbornly stuck to "There's nothing to arbitrate" and turned the matter over to the Managers Association. All the twenty-four railroads that centered in, or radiated out of, Chicago belonged to this organization. It had been formed for just such a situation, and the Managers Association looked forward to fighting it out with the ARU. Together the railroads operated 41,000 miles of track, had 221,000 employees, and possessed a combined capital of $818,000,000.

The delegates had already decided to carry the strike to the other Pullman plants. Now Debs ordered all sleeping cars to be cut from the trains and sidetracked. Switchmen of the ARU were to refuse to switch Pullman cars. If the railroads discharged the switchmen, then every other ARU worker would walk off the job, too.

The railroad officials leaped to Pullman's defense. Why, they had a contract with him! They wouldn't break a contract! They weren't going to move any train that *didn't* have sleeping cars attached.

Eugene Debs and the railroads had locked horns. . . .

"Will the AFL stand by us?" Debs wondered. He was anxious. "Will the brotherhoods help?"

He sent telegrams to find out.

Gompers of the AFL hedged. Let Debs give him full particulars, he wired back. That meant the AFL would watch from the sidelines. Some of the brotherhoods were openly hostile, others were wishy-washy in their response. Engineers *would* be allowed to take the places of engineers who quit their jobs. Conductors and brakemen would *not* walk out in sympathy with striking switchmen. The Brotherhood of Locomotive Firemen, to which Debs had given so many years and thousands of dollars of his own money, was clearly uncomfortable, but it didn't want to take any part in the strike. Its constitution prohibited the BLF from doing that, it said.

Wires sped across the country as Debs gave orders to the ARU locals: "Use no violence. Stop no trains. Select a strike committee and send me the name of the chairman."

On the third day all lines west of Chicago were stopped dead.

The Managers Association struck back by opening recruiting offices in the great cities of the East to round up strikebreakers. America was in a depression. Plenty of unemployed men jumped at the chance of working again.

38

The Biggest Strike in America

As Debs fully expected, the newspapers supported the employers. He understood why. Publishers were businessmen and were naturally on the side of the corporations. He wasn't at all surprised when the press started calling the strikers anarchists. "Best way to turn the public against us," Debs thought.

Every day a hundred to two hundred and fifty strikebreakers were recruited. They poured into Chicago. But Debs had said "no" to violence and kept repeating it: "If the railroad companies can secure men to handle their trains, they have that right. Our men have the right to quit, but their right ends there. Keep away from the railroad yards or rights of way. Respect the law!" To be sure, he couldn't be everywhere to see that his orders were carried out, and some violence, for a little while, did take place. Two express trains in Chicago were temporarily stopped. Also the Illinois Central Railroad claimed that its property in Cairo was in danger. Governor Altgeld sent militia to investigate, but the violence, if there had been any, was already over.

The U.S. district attorney in Chicago was on the side of the railroads and was not happy. Violence was what he wanted. He tried his best to bring it about. Acting as if rioters were tearing the city apart, he sent a strong telegram to Washington. The night before, he said, strikers had stopped a mail train in a Chicago suburb. Special deputies were needed. Let the U.S. marshal in Chicago hire extra deputies.

No riot of any importance had taken place. The trains that had been stopped had long ago been allowed to go on. There was no emergency whatsoever. But the newspapers kept printing horror stories, saying that the mob was in control of the city and the law was being trampled on. Frightening editorials appeared: If the

39

strikers were allowed to win, labor agitators would take control of the railroads! Debs was a dictator! Wasn't he supposed to be working against Pullman? Why, then, had he himself ridden in a Pullman car from Chicago to Terre Haute?

Debs paid no attention. He had too much to do to worry about lies. The large hall in which the workers' executive board met was filled with excited men. They ran here and there, shouted orders, asked questions. But in the midst of what looked like wildest confusion, work was being done. Press releases, telling the strikers' side of the story, were written. Appeals for help were sent. Warnings against violence were wired to the ends of the country.

The Managers Association was not idle either. They were doing their utmost to turn the public against the strike. In 1894, airplanes were only a dream and automobiles a rarity. People were largely dependent on the Iron Horse to transport them. They wanted the trains to run on time, as scheduled. The railroads purposely made the trains *not* run on time, nor as scheduled. By doing this, the Managers Association hoped that the public would protest and make the government step in. Railroads attached Pullman cars to freight trains, suburban trains, and mail trains. Maybe that would provoke the strikers to violence. If only they could be got to stop the mail trains!

It might have seemed that, with the railroads against the ARU and the brotherhoods providing strikebreakers, the odds were against the union. But Debs felt more confident now than he had at the beginning. There had never been such a strike in the United States before. More than a hundred thousand men had quit work. The strikers had succeeded in tying up all the railroads except one

40

The Biggest Strike in America

line—it was the Great Northern—between Chicago and San Francisco. The rest were paralyzed.

And the public?

The people were watching. Nearly everybody in the country was on one side or the other in this struggle between the Pullman Company and the ARU. Like people watching a football game, some chose sides without really understanding what was going on. But Debs told the railroad workers what it all meant. This was a struggle, he said, between the workers and the money power of the country. When it started, the fight was between the ARU and the Pullman Company. Then the railroads had gone into partnership with Pullman. They were standing by him while he starved his employees to death.

Who was going to win? Pullman or the ARU?

The union was holding firm, Debs said. There wasn't a sign of violence, not a single sign of disorder. The ARU had fought the railroads to a standstill. They couldn't move their trains and were losing a fortune every day. Pullman had millions behind him. The railroads were backing him. The newspapers were on his side. The ARU stood alone. Yet the union was winning.

Debs saw victory shining ahead.

7

"How Blind I Have Been!"

Eugene didn't know that he had not counted up all his enemies. Besides Pullman with his millions, besides the railroads and the press, the ARU had one foe more, stronger than all the rest. Debs had given no thought to what was going on in the government of the United States.

Down in Washington, D.C., Attorney General Richard Olney was keeping his eye on the Pullman Strike. Olney, though a hard man, was honest—honest in his own way. Like Debs, he wanted justice. But his idea of justice was totally different. Debs regarded a strike as a blow for freedom, the use of the one great weapon the working class had against oppression. No greedy employer had ever oppressed Richard Olney. To him a strike was a great act of violence. Whether or not strikers were violent *during* a strike was not the point. The great violence was the strike itself. He regarded a strike as an unlawful act by many people. In other words, it was a rebellion. A rebellion had to be crushed. And the way to crush it was to bring all the force possible to bear upon it.

Attorney General Olney had been a corporation lawyer representing railroads. A few years before the Pullman strike, he had been on the board of one of the railroads that was now fighting the ARU. His sympathy was on the side of the railroads. As he saw it, it was his duty to crush the Pullman strike. Certainly nobody else could be trusted to do it. Chicago's Mayor Hopkins had contributed meat and flour for the Pullman strikers. Governor Altgeld of Illinois had pardoned the Haymarket anarchists. It was up to him, Richard Olney. He would secure a federal injunction against the strike. Then he would get President Cleveland to send U.S. troops to Chicago to enforce the court order. Crushing force—that was the way to do it.

On July 2, the ARU received an unexpected blow. Judge Peter Grosscup and Judge William A. Woods of the federal court in Chicago issued an injunction against the ARU leaders. The court forbade them to do anything to aid the strike. They couldn't send telegrams. They couldn't give orders or answer questions. They couldn't speak to workers and urge them to join the strike.

Heavy thoughts passed through the minds of Debs and his comrades. If they obeyed, the strike was finished and the ARU destroyed. Thousands of ARU men would be unemployed. Not only that. Throughout the country workers would suffer because employers, having crushed the ARU, would immediately turn against every trade union.

44

"How Blind I Have Been!"

What a price to pay for helping Pullman's starving workers! What should be done?

Debs went to see one of the best constitutional lawyers in Chicago, Clarence Darrow, attorney for the Chicago and Northwestern Railroad. On the surface, the choice of Darrow might have seemed strange. But Debs knew Darrow was not only a brilliant lawyer but one who sympathized with labor. Darrow often spoke at radical meetings and had taken a leading part in the amnesty campaign for the Haymarket anarchists.

Darrow examined the injunction and said: "Proceed just as you have been doing. You are not committing violence; you are not advising violence."

The ARU leaders proceeded. The injunction was illegal, unconstitutional, the lawyer had said so, and the ARU would fight it. They would take their chances of going to jail.

On the third of July, after a wearing day at the ARU headquarters, Debs went to his hotel very late. As usual, his brother Theodore was with him, for the brothers were inseparable. They went up to their room but had slept only a few hours when they were awakened by the sound of bugles under their window.

"It's the Fourth of July," thought Eugene. "There's a parade."

Getting out of bed, he walked to the window. He could hardly believe his eyes! Right under his window and all along the lake front, U.S. soldiers were encamped.

"What does it mean?" Debs asked himself. Why had the president sent troops to Chicago? Federal troops were to help out only when a situation was so violent that it could not be handled by the state militia. But the militia had not been used!

Debs didn't know that Attorney General Olney was pulling strings behind the scenes. Judge Grosscup and others of Olney's accomplices in Chicago had sent him just the telegram he needed. It said that there was grave violence in the city. Actually the violence had occurred not in Chicago itself but in a suburb, where strikers, acting against Debs's strict orders, were said to have stopped mail trains. Actually the disburbance—if there had been any—had been brief and was already over. Of this nothing appeared in the telegram. On the contrary, the wire said that nothing less than the U.S. Army could control the riotous situation in Chicago. Olney had immediately spoken to the president, and the president had immediately sent federal troops from Fort Sheridan "to preserve order and protect private property."

Something happened to Debs when he saw the U.S. soldiers under his window. For a moment he was confused. Then his mind cleared and he understood.

Long ago, in the days when he was working for the BLF, he had insisted that there was no such thing as class conflict between those who owned the factories and mines and those who sweated to earn their bread. He had said that anybody who believed in such a conflict between capital and labor was a very shallow thinker. Now, in the flash of every bayonet, he saw how shallow had been his own thinking. It seemed clear to him that the federal government was on the side of the owners of wealth. The president had not said one harsh word against Pullman or the railroads. But he had sent troops to shoot down peacefully striking workers!

Debs was all the more bitter because the president who had sent the soldiers was Grover Cleveland. Debs had been a Democrat

"How Blind I Have Been!"

all his life. Three times he had campaigned for Grover Cleveland. And now!

"How blind I have been!" Eugene thought. "In a struggle between workers and corporations, neither a Democratic nor a Republican president will ever be impartial. Both will act on the side of big business."

Quickly he got ready to go to the ARU headquarters. "It is wrong," he said to his brother. "The soldiers will not serve to keep the peace. Instead, they will be the signal for civil war. There is going to be bloodshed."

Governor Altgeld was even angrier than Debs about the Federal troops. Mincing no words, he wired Cleveland that so long as the Illinois militia was able to take care of a violent situation, the federal government had no business to interfere. The governor had not asked for help. None was needed. The newspapers were giving out false reports. The mail trains *were* going through. It was true that the railroads couldn't move some of their trains. But that was not because the strikers were violent. It was because the railroads couldn't get men to operate their trains for them. The president was going beyond his powers. He had a swollen idea of what his powers were. Altgeld asked Cleveland to withdraw the troops.

The president brushed the governor aside.

And now the bloodshed Debs had predicted began. It looked very much as if the soldiers were trying to provoke violence. On July 5 they made a bayonet charge against a crowd and injured several people. But the special deputies whom the federal marshal had turned loose on the city were even worse. Given pistols and the freedom to shoot, they used their weapons as if playing cops and

47

robbers. On one occasion they fired into a group of people when there was absolutely no reason to do so. Another time a man was simply looking on while hoodlums were overturning freight cars. He was a hundred yards from the riot when a deputy shot him. As the wounded man was trying to get up, the deputy shot him again and killed him. Special deputies had actually been hired to incite disorder, not put it down, and these thieves, thugs, and ex-convicts were performing to the complete satisfaction of the railroads.

There were fires, great fires. The alarm bells tolled, people were terrified, and the press made the most of the confusion. Screaming conspiracy, treason, and murder, the newspapers blamed the strikers for setting the fires. This was not true. Indeed, the fire department found several deputy marshals cutting the firehoses so that the fires could not be put out. Nor did the railroads seem to care anything about the loss of their old coaches. To all appearances, they were pleased to have them burned so they could collect insurance on them.

What with the soldiers and the special deputies, Debs had new worries. The newspapers announced that there was WILD RIOT IN CHICAGO and that the mob was THIRSTY FOR BLOOD. The press claimed the strikers were on the warpath and threatened to destroy every living thing. A cry went up: "Down with the ARU! Down with anarchy!"

Debs was meantime busy appealing to strikers to be orderly and to abide by the law. Having decided to pay no attention to the injunction, the ARU leaders were moving quietly from one open-air meeting to another and urging strikers to use no violence.

"Stand fast!" the leaders said to the strikers. "Keep away from the railroad lines!"

48

"How Blind I Have Been!"

And to the local unions Debs wired: "Every true man must quit now and remain out until the fight is won. Men must be for us or against us. Our cause is gaining ground daily and our success is only a question of a few days. Do not falter in this hour! Stand erect! Proclaim your manhood! Labor must win now or never!"

On July 10 things came to a head. At the request of the Managers Association a federal grand jury met in Chicago to decide whether the strike leaders should be indicted for conspiracy to interfere with interstate commerce.

The ARU had sent out 900 telegrams. The Federal Court of Chicago made the telegraph companies hand them over. Out of the total, 150 telegrams were selected and many were read aloud to the grand jury. One telegram only had any hint of violence in it, and this one had been sent by an excited youngster while Debs himself was away from headquarters. Many telegrams, on the other hand, had counseled against violence. Nevertheless, on the evidence of the telegrams alone, Debs and his three top officers were indicted. They were arrested, but were released on bail.

The strike was broken now. Trains along most of the lines were moving. With a heavy heart Debs appeared at a meeting of the AFL and other national unions and asked Gompers to go and see the Managers Association. Let him say that Debs would call off the strike if all the ARU members would be rehired.

Gompers refused. He would go together with Debs, but not alone.

What good was that? Debs knew the railroads would not meet with him.

Mayor Hopkins finally carried the offer to the Managers Association. But the railroads had long before met in secret and had agreed not to rehire the strikers. The answer the mayor brought back was "no."

Debs wouldn't admit to himself that everything was over. He kept sending out telegrams to bolster up the strikers. He let himself dream that in the Far West the union might still win.

It was a forlorn hope. On July 17, Eugene, his two top officers, and five other strike leaders were arrested for not obeying the injunction. Much to the surprise of the judge, they decided not to accept bail.

"It is a matter of principle," Debs said when he was asked about it. "The poor striker who is arrested would be thrown in jail. We are no better than he."

Anyway, what was the use of being out now? The Pullman strike was lost.

8

Thoughts in Jail

The next six days were to be the hardest Eugene had ever experienced. It wasn't that he brooded about the lost strike. As always, he went on to the next thing, but the next thing now was the Cook County Jail. In the years to come, Eugene would say, "So long as there is a soul in prison, *I* am not free." In the Cook County Jail he was already beginning to feel that way.

He had not even been aware—in the hurly-burly of the strike—of what lay behind the grim, stone walls of the city jail. With shock, Eugene took in the slits of grimy, barred windows high in the walls; the floor covered with slime and tobacco spit; the mildewed straw mattresses crawling with vermin; the gloom; the sewer rats. In this prison, he was to learn, the Haymarket martyrs had been kept for eighteen months. Here they were hanged.

Eugene found himself locked in a cell with five other men. Bunks, three high, stood against the walls. Half-naked men sat or lay on these bunks and scratched themselves till blood trickled in tiny rivulets down their bodies. For twenty hours a day they were at liberty to do this. The other four—two in the morning, two in the afternoon—they could walk around and around in the corridors. Eugene wanted to read, but there was no light except what trickled in from the screened globe outside the door. At night it was impossible to sleep on account of the sobbing and screaming that came from the fifty or more women imprisoned on the other side of the wall.

For once Eugene had more than enough time to think. He thought about his companions, who had not yet been convicted of crime and were only waiting to be tried. He thought of justice. He thought of freedom, which meant a better life for all. He thought of *Les Miserables* and the terrible prison in which Jean Valjean had spent nineteen years. Like his hero, the miserable beings in this jail were being ground up in what now, for the first time, Debs began to call "the system."

Some time before the Pullman strike, he had read *The Cooperative Commonwealth*, a book by Lawrence Gronlund. Gronlund believed that factories and mines should not be operated in order to make the owners rich. Rather they should be owned by the people and be operated in the interests of the people.

Could this really be done? If it were, there need never be another strike! Gronlund called his good society *socialism*. Could a dedicated band of socialists lead the nation to that good society?

52

Thoughts in Jail

Gronlund thought so. Debs wasn't sure. He kept saying to himself: "in the interest of the people and not for private gain." The words sounded radiant with promise.

Debs thought of another book he had been enthusiastic about at the time he read it. It was by Edward Bellamy and was called *Looking Backward*. It was the story of a young man who falls asleep and wakes up in the year 2,000. He is astonished by what he sees. In the society in which he finds himself, factories are run not for private profit but in the interest of the people. Looking backward at his own society, he is shocked by the ugliness, the ignorance, the greed, the oppression, the few rich, the many poor.

To describe conditions in the nineteenth century, Bellamy drew an unforgettable picture. He compared the society of his own day to a heavy coach being dragged uphill. The driver of the coach was Hunger. With cruel indifference he lashed the many ragged, starving men, women, and children who, with all their strength, were pulling at the rope. They stumbled, they fell in the mire, they died. The driver gave no heed. Meanwhile on top of the coach rode a few well-dressed, well-fed passengers. They cared nothing for those who strained at the rope. The only concern of those riding on top was that by some mischance they might fall off. For then they would immediately have to take hold of the rope and pull.

It was horrifying to think of a society organized like this. But Eugene Debs had to admit that the picture was shockingly true. He thought of the starving workers in Pullman. He thought of the strikers who at this very moment were vainly seeking work while their families struggled with want. He thought of little children feeding machines ten hours a day while the machines starved them. Looking about him at the wretched prisoners, Debs fancied their past. He saw them pulling at the rope, panting, falling in the mire.

Could not society be organized in some better way?

Not for an instant was Debs sorry for having disobeyed the injunction. Though the strike had been lost, he was convinced that he and his comrades had done the right thing to carry on. The strike had served a great purpose. It had called the attention of the whole country to the fact that the owners of wealth enslaved the workers. The strike was a step toward freeing men from slavery and degradation.

Debs and the other leaders of the ARU had been ready to accept any punishment rather than obey. But after six days in the Cook County Jail, they were happy to learn that the hearings of their case were postponed to September 5 and that for the time being they could be free on bond. This time they accepted it, and Eugene went home to Terre Haute.

How good it was to be back with Kate! How good to have a clean bed and food he enjoyed! What a comfort to see his parents! He had always tried to be at their house on Sunday night and sometimes traveled hundreds of miles to be with them. All through the strike he had written or wired every day. On July 18, one week after the jury had indicted him, he had received a telegram from them. "Stand by your principles regardless of consequences," the wire had said. It was signed: "Your Mother and Father."

He and his parents were very close. . . .

But glad as he was to be home, the strain of the strike and the distress he felt about the prisoners had been too much for Eugene. He fell ill and had to spend two weeks in bed. Lovingly Kate nursed him. Never once did she complain of her lonely life, nor reproach him for being so prodigal of his health. That was the kind of man he was, and she was proud of him. She patched him up and got him ready for the next bout.

In September, Federal Judge William A. Woods sentenced Debs to six months in jail for failing to obey the injunction. Eugene's sentence was to be twice as long as those of his seven comrades because the judge considered him a dangerous man and a menace to society. The defense lawyers at once appealed to the U.S. Supreme Court, and meantime the ARU men were free on bond.

But there was also the conspiracy trial ahead of them. It opened on January 8. The Cook County Jail being too crowded, the strike leaders were held in the McHenry County Jail in Woodstock, fifty-four miles from Chicago. Throughout the trial, which lasted nearly a month, the ARU men were brought every day from the jail in Woodstock to the courtroom in Chicago.

Debs had no intention of letting the trial take place in the dark. The whole thing was infamous, he told the press. There wasn't a scrap of evidence to show that any of the indicted men had broken any law.

Defense lawyer Clarence Darrow agreed with Debs. There was no evidence of guilt. Except for one executive meeting, all the ARU convention meetings had been open to reporters. And after the Pullman strike began, the union held no secret meetings. On the other hand, how about the Managers Association? What had happened at *their* meetings?

Thus, cleverly, did the ARU counsel turn the conspiracy trial into an attack on the railroads.

55

Put on the stand, the general managers lied. They said they "could not remember" what happened. But Darrow had got hold of the minutes of a managers' meeting. At this meeting the railroads had openly conspired with the Pullman Company to stand together and destroy the ARU.

Debs charged the managers with perjury. They were not indicted. George Pullman was summoned to appear in court. He had his palace car attached to a New York train and went east.

By this time the managers sensed that the trial was going against them. They could see the effect of the evidence on the jury. It was the managers' good luck—or was this contrived by them?—that one of the jurors fell ill. Seizing the opportunity, the judge dismissed the jury and announced that the case would be continued on the first Monday in May.

The jury were no sooner dismissed than they came pouring from the jury box to congratulate the defendants—it was clear as day that the case was a frame-up! They found Debs stunned by the sudden turn the trial had taken. He wanted to fight the case through and clear his name. There was good reason, he thought, to believe that the trial would never be reopened.

However, nothing could be done. So the ARU leaders shook hands all around and left for their respective homes.

9

Six Months

Debs and his comrades were not to stay out of jail long. The Supreme Court turned down the appeal on the injunction, and the ARU men were sent to Woodstock to serve their sentences.

Though the McHenry County Jail was not far from Chicago, it was worlds away from the gloomy place in which Debs had spent six such painful days. The Woodstock jail was merely a few cells in the sheriff's own house. As for the sheriff, he was one in a million. Having come to know Debs and some of the other men before, he decided that the prisoners were not criminals and should not be treated as such. He let them eat with his own family, play football in the street behind the jail, and read books in the jail library. Had they not been locked in their cells at night, Eugene and his companions would have had no sense of being imprisoned.

After the Pullman strike, Debs was a celebrity. Jailed, he was doubly a celebrity. Reporters from newspapers, large and small, came to interview him. Visitors came. Mail poured in from everywhere. It swamped the Woodstock post office so that Eugene had to hire a secretary to help him answer his letters. In one two-week period he received 1,500 letters. Some were from cranks. Most were from important people. And only one letter really provoked him.

This was a notice from the Justice Department saying that his application for a pardon was being considered. Pardon? He had never applied for a pardon. Debs wrote back indignantly that he was entitled to his freedom as a matter of justice and refused to accept it as a matter of mercy.

Never was any jail term less dreary. What with good food, books, letters, and football, the prisoners scarcely noticed the passing of time. Three months went by and all but Debs were released. Bidding them a cheerful good-bye, Eugene knew they wouldn't be idle long. They would throw themselves into rebuilding the union, which was in pieces after the Pullman strike. Many of the railroad workers who had quit their jobs were still unemployed. Low as the dues were, the members could not pay them. Indeed, things were so bad with the union that the Chicago office had been closed. The ARU had moved to Terre Haute and established its headquarters in the house which in 1889, mainly out of money Kate had inherited from an aunt, Eugene and his wife had built for themselves.

As soon as Eugene's fellow prisoners had gone, Kate Debs arrived in Woodstock—to stay, she announced, until her husband was released. She settled herself in the town, arranged for board with the sheriff's family, and that same day began to help Eugene with his correspondence. There were some people in Terre Haute who had never stopped wondering why Eugene had picked out Kate Metzel for a wife. She seemed so cold and distant. They would have understood if they could have seen her working by her husband's side or taking over the letters entirely and leaving Eugene free to edit the ARU *Railway Times*. Kate and Eugene had no children—she could not have any. Kate's fulfillment came from standing by her husband. Whatever suited him suited her.

Eugene had nothing to complain of now. Yet he chafed. He missed the sense of the firing line to which he had so long been accustomed. He longed to be out there, helping workingmen to get a fair day's pay for a fair day's work.

He didn't suspect that he was soon going to see things in an entirely different way. . . .

Socialists had written long letters to him, hoping to win him to their views. They had sent him books and pamphlets and had patiently explained to him the ideas of Karl Marx. Victor Berger—a school teacher from Milwaukee—had paid Debs a visit and had left him a book by the famous thinker. Eugene didn't read it—Karl Marx seemed dull. He thought about socialism but couldn't make up his mind about it.

At the same time he could not accept a society ruled by the big corporations. He rejected the spirit of dog eat dog, of each for himself and the devil take the hindmost. He detested what he now pictured to himself as a few rich people riding luxuriously on top of a coach that the many poor struggled to drag uphill. But he was not a radical. He had not yet done with trying to reform the system. He yearned for justice but was not yet persuaded that justice would prevail only if society was built on an entirely different plan. And yet the words of Gronlund haunted him: "in the interest of the people and not for private gain."

As November 22 approached, Debs became more and more eager to get out. And now the day of release had come. He had heard that a reception was being planned for him in Chicago and that a special train would arrive at five o'clock to carry him to the city. His books and clothes were packed. He was dressed and ready. In jail his face had filled out, and he looked splendid in the new black suit Kate had bought for him.

By the time the special train with fifty union delegates aboard could be seen approaching Woodstock, ten thousand people were at the station. The train ground to a stop. The passengers saw Debs and made for their hero. They cheered and laughed and cried and kissed him in the sight of the ten thousand.

In Chicago ten times the number filled the station and the streets around it. A hundred thousand people went wild when they saw Debs. Here was the man who had never let them down! He had let the strikers into bloodless battle, had stood up to the railroads, the newspapers, the federal courts, the U.S. Army. Nothing had bowled him over. He had gone to jail for the union! He had been true!

Debs was lifted to sturdy shoulders. Inch by inch his bearers forced their way through the crowd toward the Armory. A carriage drawn by six white horses stood waiting, but it waited in vain —Debs would not get in.

"If the rest walk, I shall walk, too," he insisted. "What is good enough for them is also good enough for me."

Six Months

There were welcoming speeches in the hall. The millionaire reporter Henry Demarest Lloyd, always on labor's side, spoke against the injunction that had sent Debs to jail. Governor Waite of Colorado spoke—he had never forgotten that he had been a miner. Then Eugene got up. The thing uppermost in his mind was the conspiracy trial, which had never reopened. He said he wanted to clear his name, then went on to speak of liberty and how people must fight to hold on to it. His voice was magnificent, his presence radiant. They carried to everyone there the feeling that this man was for them. When he had finished and left the hall, the whole audience burst into song—they would "Hang Judge Woods to a Sour Apple Tree!"

Back in Terre Haute, Eugene was shocked to find his father grown so old. Daniel had now retired from business. He was in his middle seventies and nearly blind. It was distressing to come home and find the sturdy oak against which he had leaned so shaky. As never before, Eugene realized what the relationship meant to him.

It had meant all the more because, for all that he was so popular in Terre Haute, Eugene had always shrunk from formal society. His evenings were spent nearly always at home, alone with Kate or with some good guest like the poet James Whitcomb Riley, who always stayed at the Debs home when he came to town. And Sundays Eugene was always at his parents' home.

But there was little time now to do the loving things he wanted to do for his father. Immediate ARU problems had to be faced. The union owed more than $30,000 for lawyers and printing.

Not long after he came home, Eugene dropped into the office of printer Thaddeus Moore and without a word passed a paper across his desk. Moore looked up, puzzled. The paper was a deed to Debs's house.

"That's partial payment on the ARU debt," Eugene explained.

"But you don't owe the debt personally!" Moore protested.

"Lock it up in your safe just the same," Eugene said.

He was taking responsibility for all the ARU debts. Eugene could not bear to owe money to anyone, and his plans were all made. After the Pullman strike, the whole country knew his name. He would travel from town to town, hire a hall, announce that Eugene V. Debs would speak, and people would pay to hear him.

It was to take him eighteen years, but Eugene paid back every dollar the union owed.

10

"I Am for Socialism Because I Am for Humanity."

As the months passed, Eugene found himself floundering. He grasped at one "solution" after another.

It was not that he didn't understand the problem. The problem was clear enough: workers wanted higher wages and employers wanted higher profits. How could the two be reconciled?

Back in 1885, Eugene had been elected by the Democratic party to serve a term in the Indiana legislature. He had felt totally frustrated on that job because when he wanted to serve labor, he found his hands tied. He had sensed then that those who owned the nation's wealth controlled the men in government. Since that time, the Pullman strike had impressed the same idea on him—only more positively. Debs had come to believe that the government served the corporations: when the going got rough, it stepped in on the side of big business. And as for the courts, money talked: the judicial nets were so adjusted as to the catch the minnows and let the whales slip through.

Eugene Debs, who looked so sweet-faced and mild, so like a preacher in his gold-rimmed eyeglasses, was a fighter. He had gone to jail because he would not abandon the cause of the common man. But he was coming to feel that the common man held the key to his freedom in his own hands. He had the vote, didn't he? Let him cast it for freedom!

There was a party called the People's party. Like the Democrats and the Republicans, it was a capitalist party. Nevertheless, it stood for industrial unions—classless unions like his ARU. Debs believed in industrial unions; he held they were a step in the right direction. Henry Demarest Lloyd wanted him to run for president on the People's party ticket. Eugene was of two minds about that. He considered himself a servant of the people, yet—"I have absolutely no political ambition whatever," he answered Lloyd, hedging. The truth was that after his experience with Grover Cleveland, he didn't want to be tied to *any* capitalist party. He thought the matter through, talked with Kate about it, then sent Lloyd another wire: "Please do not permit use of my name for nomination."

But since he believed in industrial unions, he wanted to help. Debs made twenty speeches in support of the candidate. To his disgust, the election turned out to be a clean sweep for the Republicans. McKinley was to be the next president.

What was the matter with the people that they could give the Republicans a landslide victory? No sane man could be satisfied

Campaign poster, 1900. Debs's first try for the Presidency

"I Am for Socialism Because I Am for Humanity."

with the way things were. Why did workers vote against their own interests?

The matter was, Debs decided, that big business was in control of more than business. Through the press, it controlled the minds of the people. It befuddled the common man into thinking that what was good for big business was good for him. "The capitalist press is the mouthpiece of the owners of wealth," Debs declared.

He was of the common people. But he had come a long way in his thinking. He had passed, as he put it, "from midnight darkness to the noontide light of day." After that landslide election, he realized that he was through with reforms as a solution. Reforms alone would never bring about a just society. Had Tom Paine been a reformer? Had Patrick Henry? Had John Brown? Debs drew strength from the great radicals in American History. He no longer backed away from sweeping change. Men were made to be brothers. They were meant to cooperate with their fellows, not try to get ahead of them. Eugene wanted an America in which people cooperated, in which the factories and mines were run not to make a few men rich but to create abundance for the people. A struggle was coming. It would be between capitalism and socialism, between the oppressor and the oppressed, and in that struggle he knew which side he was on.

"I am for socialism because I am for humanity," he wrote in the *Railway Times*. It was January 1897. The time had come, he said, for a new society to be born.

On October 1, 1898, the Social Democratic party, sprung from the ashes of the ARU, opened its headquarters in Chicago. It

65

was a tiny party, laughably small. In the whole city there were perhaps no more than fifteen socialists. But Debs was on the Party's executive board, and his eyes were on the future. What did small beginnings matter when the future was theirs?

The office was a modest one. Rent for the one-room head-quarters was ten dollars a month. Theodore Debs, now married and with his wife by his side, was treasurer. It was his duty to pay out the rent. But often the ten dollars was not on hand, and then he had to borrow it from one of the two lawyers who were on the party's executive board. If neither of these gentlemen could oblige, Theodore would pawn his watch. Once the treasury was down to two dollars.

Nevertheless Debs believed that his party—it was to be called the Socialist party in 1901—was off to a good start. Anyway, according to his thinking, it had no blinkers on its eyes. It saw clearly that there were two classes in society and that one class—the capitalists, the owners of wealth—oppressed the other class, who did the work. The Party held that the capitalist system was rotten through and through and could not be reformed. Socialism was going to sweep it away and start fresh. Under socialism, workers would no longer have to plead for a fair day's pay for a fair day's work. The goal of the Party was to *scrap the wage system* altogether. There would be cooperation in industry. The factories, the railroads, the mines, and the banks would be owned by the people and run by the workers themselves. Of course, it would take socialists a long time to reach that goal. But wasn't it better to go slowly along the right road than to speed along the wrong one?

Debs felt he had come to a sign post that pointed two ways.

66

"I Am for Socialism Because I Am for Humanity."

One arrow pointed to *Capitalism, Total Slavery*. That road was a well-paved highway. The other arrow pointed to *Socialism, Complete Freedom*. The road was narrow, muddy, stony, rough. He had chosen the difficult road. Sometimes he wondered why he had stood hesitating at the signpost so long. Now that he had taken the first steps, he was determined that all the working class should choose the same road. Complete Freedom! What a goal!

Traveling through the country lecturing, teaching people about socialism, never denying that the road was rough, always sure that socialism was the only road to freedom, Debs was encouraged by the fact that the Party did not stand alone. It had the support of several small newspapers and of one that was soon to have 100,000 subscribers—the *Appeal to Reason*. Its publisher was Julius Wayland, an ex-printer who had established himself in the little town of Girard, Kansas. The *Appeal to Reason* was only a four-page sheet. It came out only once a week. But it spoke out strongly for socialism. Wherever Debs went on his lecture tours, he found farmers and workingmen reading the *Appeal to Reason*. Socialism was a small light. But it was bright and it was spreading.

Debs believed he had had a good opportunity during the Pullman strike to see how the capitalist system worked in times of peace. In 1898 he got a chance, he said, to see how it operated in a time of war.

War, in his eyes, was large-scale murder. It solved—for a time—some problems for the big corporations. But it never benefitted the working class. And now the newspapers were calling for war with Spain. Why?

To a socialist the reason was clear. The American frontier had practically disappeared. The big corporations needed raw materials and new markets for their goods. Big business was looking with greedy eyes to the Spanish colonies in the Caribbean and the Pacific. A successful war with Spain would give big business what it wanted. So the newspapers were trying to befuddle people's minds.

It takes courage to talk against war when the newspapers are whipping it up. Debs spoke out. He said that the victims of war were always the poor. No matter how a war turned out, the result for the workers was always bad. Socialists were opposed to war, he told his audiences. "But if it ever becomes necessary for us to enlist in the murderous business, it will be to wipe out capitalism." Capitalism, Debs said, was the enemy of the oppressed and downtrodden of all nations.

The war craze did not sweep Debs off his feet. When the American battleship *Maine* mysteriously exploded in Havana harbor, killing hundreds of American sailors, and the newspapers screamed, "Remember the *Maine*!" Debs stood firm. And when at the war's end the United States annexed the Philippines, he denounced the act. The big corporations were getting the raw materials and the markets they wanted, he said. But they were getting them by force of arms and "at the expense of the lives of a people whose only offense had been love of freedom."

In 1898 it was still possible to speak out against war in wartime and get away with it.

11

Arouse, Ye Slaves!

Eugene Debs led a hard life speaking for socialism. Anybody else would have found it unendurable to make seven speeches a week, months on end, each speech two hours long. Who would choose to travel a thousand miles a week in dirty day coaches? Who would sleep in strange beds, eat tasteless food, and seldom get home to see his family and friends—all for one hundred dollars a month? But Eugene did it and liked it. Speaking was his craft, and he got satisfaction out of being an artist at it. He was on fire with a vision of a world in which people would cooperate instead of tearing at one another's throats. If only the working class would use their eyes and see; their ears and hear; their brains and think! How soon the earth could be made to blossom with beauty and joy!

"You produce the wealth," he told workers. "You ought to be, and can be, the master of the earth."

Under capitalism, he told his audiences, workers were no more than slaves. "You are as much subject to the command of the capitalist," Debs said, "as if you were his property under the law. You have got to go to his factory because you have to work. He is the master of your job, and you cannot work without his consent. And he only gives this on condition that you surrender to him all you produce except what is necessary to keep you in running order."

Capitalists couldn't get along without workers, Debs said. But workers did not need the capitalist. There was nothing they could not do for themeslves. However, they must study to fit themselves to take control. Instead of being simply cogs, every worker must hold up his head. He must look over the whole mechanism and see his relation to every other worker in the industry. Then, when the revolution came, the working class could take over.

Debs was confident he was getting across, for the Socialist party was growing. In 1900 he ran for President and polled 100,000 votes. In the 1904 election he got four times as many.

This is not to say that there were no conflicts in the Socialist party. There were. Debs thought that all unions should be revolutionary. He insisted that while workers fought for higher wages, they must never forget that the socialist goal was to do away with the wage system altogether. But many skilled workers were forgetting about the goal. They were interested in the here and now.

Debs didn't trust Gompers. Eugene felt that Gompers was

70

THE WORKING CLASS CANDIDATE
FOR PRESIDENT

EUGENE V. DEBS
OF INDIANA

WILL DISCUSS THE ISSUES OF THE NATIONAL CAMPAIGN AT

WASHINGTON HALL
18th STREET CORNER HARNEY

Sunday, October 9th, 8 P. M.
ADMISSION 10 CENTS

JOHN F. HIDDING PRINT

Broadside announcing campaign speech, 1904

Arouse, Ye Slaves!

hand in glove with the employers. How could it be otherwise when he banquetted with millionaires? As if there was something in common between them! There was nothing in common between capitalists and workingmen. Their interests were not the same although Gompers kept saying they were. Wolves might sit down at the same board with the sheep, but by and by the wolves would fleece and devour the sheep.

Debs believed that of all the groups in America there was only one that could lead the battle against capitalism. That was the working class. "As individual slaves," he told the workers, "you are helpless, and your condition is hopeless. As a class you are the greatest power between the earth and the stars."

He wasn't a Moses, he said, who would lead them into the Promised Land. "If I could lead you in, someone else could lead you out." It was up to themselves. Debs said that a new labor federation was absolutely necessary, one that included the skilled and the unskilled.

He wasn't the only socialist who believed it. There were many socialists in the Western Federation of Miners who saw eye to eye with him. In 1904, under the leadership of Bill Haywood and Charles Moyer, the Western Federation of Miners made plans to unite all workers into one big union. This union was to be called the *Industrial Workers of the World*. It would have that name because it would be open to any worker in a foreign country who held a union card. The leaders had not forgotten that Karl Marx, the great socialist thinker, had said: "Workers of all countries, unite. You have nothing to lose but your chains. You have a world to gain."

Eugene heartily approved of the IWW. Like himself, the

71

IWW believed in the class struggle and wasn't afraid to talk about it. As soon as the IWW was organized, Debs joined it. But Gompers was frightened; he didn't like the competition. Indeed, there were many differences of opinion among labor people. Some supported one group, some another. There seemed to be nothing that labor could agree on. Then something happened that brought the working class together: Charles Moyer, president of the Western Federation of Miners, Bill Haywood, its secretary-treasurer, and George Pettibone, a Denver businessman, were indicted for murder.

The case was this:

On the 30th of December, 1905, Frank Steunenberg, former Governor of Idaho, was killed by a bomb. It had exploded just as he opened the gate of his home at Caldwell, Idaho. Harry Orchard, a member of the Western Federation of Miners, was arrested on suspicion. Two weeks later he made a confession. He said that Moyer, Haywood, and Pettibone had hired him to kill Steunenberg. Orchard said that the motive for the murder was revenge. During the Coeur d'Alene strike in the lead and silver country, Governor Steunenberg had called out the militia.

A month after the confession, a secret complaint was filed in Idaho against Moyer, Haywood, and Pettibone. But since the men were all residents of Denver, they had to be extradited to Idaho to be tried. The governor of Colorado cooperated. He secretly signed the necessary papers, the three men were put on a special train under heavy guard and were taken to Idaho, where they were indicted for murder.

The Pinkerton detective who got the confession out of Harry Orchard let fall some interesting things. He told a newspaper reporter that the indicted men "would never leave Idaho alive." He said also that even if they were acquitted, they would be convicted in Colorado. He had "information and proof," he said, "of their connection with a dozen atrocious murders in Colorado."

Debs's mind flashed back to Chicago and the eight Haymarket anarchists. "All this is to silence every cry for a fair trial!" he thought. If there was one thing he was sure of, it was that he was not going to let another such frame-up happen.

Why was Pettibone arrested? Clearly the Denver businessman, though he had once been active in the Western Federation of Miners, was just a blind. He was not important. He was arrested only to hide the real reason for the indictments. The real reason, Debs decided, was an attempt to destroy the Western Federation of Miners and the IWW.

"If they hang Haywood and Moyer, they'll have to hang me," Debs told his friends. And before twenty-four hours were up, he had a "call to workers" in the office of the *Appeal to Reason*.

The socialist paper had a quarter of a million subscribers now. But this time it came out in a special edition of *four million* copies. The headline on the first page read:

AROUSE, YE SLAVES!

Under it was Debs's "call." "Murder has been plotted and is about to be executed in the name of law." The indictments of

Moyer, Haywood, and Pettibone were "a foul plot; a damnable conspiracy; a hellish outrage."

The Pinkerton man had said the men would never leave Idaho alive. "Well, by the gods," Debs wrote, "if they do not, the governors of Idaho and Colorado and the masters from Wall Street, New York to the Rocky Mountains had better prepare to follow them."

If an attempt was made to repeat the Haymarket tragedy, there would be revolution, Debs warned, and he would do all in his power to start it.

"They have done their best and their worst to crush and enslave us," Debs wrote. "Their politicians have betrayed us, their courts have thrown us into jail without trial, and their soldiers have shot our comrades dead in their tracks. Let them dare to execute their devilish plot and every state in the Union will resound with the tramp of revolution.

"Get ready, comrades, for action! No other course is left to the working class."

The threat of revolution didn't stop the courts. The wheels of "justice" ground on, and from day to day the outlook for the indicted men looked darker.

"If we cannot arouse the people sufficiently to threaten revolt on a large scale, they are gone," Debs warned in the *Appeal to Reason*. "Nothing else can save them."

The whole labor movement rallied to the cause of Moyer and Haywood. Hundreds of protest meetings were held. In the large cities, huge protest parades took place. In Boston, fifty thousand people marched in the streets, chanting:

74

Arouse, Ye Slaves!

If Moyer and Haywood die; if Moyer and Haywood die,
Twenty million workingmen will know the reason why.

Debs told the people that the trial was "the greatest legal battle in history."

Weeks passed. The tension kept growing. At ten o'clock on a Saturday evening the Haywood case was given to the jury. There was no radio or television in those days, and the streets of Boise were filled with people waiting to hear the verdict. The court was jammed. At seven in the morning, word came that the jury had agreed. In the breathless stillness of the courtroom, the verdict was pronounced: "Not guilty!"

When the *Appeal to Reason* came out on August 3, it printed what its readers already knew and were rejoicing about. In huge red letters across the black print of its usual front page were the words:

NOT
GUILTY

12

The Red Special

In the spring of 1906, in the midst of the campaign to free Moyer and Haywood, a heavy personal blow struck Eugene—his mother died. He went home at once. He tried to stifle his grief so as to be able to comfort his father, who was now eighty-six years old and blind. But Daniel was beyond comforting. Daisy had been his wife for fifty-seven years. They had had ten children and watched four of them die. A few months after Daisy, he also passed away.

The double loss was hard for Eugene to accept, for his parents had been more to him than he could sum up in words. He was wont to say that he owed everything to socialism. Sometimes he said sentimentally that Kate had been the great inspiration of his life. He knew better. It was in his childhood home that he had been turned toward seeking justice, it was there that he had learned the meaning of freedom. All that he was, all that he was able to feel and give, reached back to the two-story frame house with its grocery store, to the devotion of his mother, to the talks with his father, to the books in that home. Eugene Debs remembered everything—with love and gratitude.

By the time the campaign of 1908 got on the way—with Debs as presidential candidate for the third time—Eugene was fifty-two years old. He suffered from rheumatism, lumbago, headache. On top of that and the recent loss of his parents, he had had a bitter disappointment:

While the battle to free the indicted men was going on, the IWW, on which he had set such high hopes, had been almost destroyed. Haywood was in jail for fifteen months. During that time his enemies had taken over the leadership of the Western Federation of Miners and had withdrawn the union from the IWW. After that the IWW ceased to be a trade union in the sense of guiding workers day to day. The IWW turned against government itself. Now it regarded socialist politics as being no better than capitalist politics. The members of the IWW were carried away by the idea that trade unions themselves should run the country.

Debs thought this nonsense. Socialism was the core of all his thinking. He let his dues in the IWW lapse and ceased to be a member.

With all this dragging him down, Eugene Debs was not the flaming figure he had been. But once he began to campaign, he snapped back into form. Every soul in his audiences felt that Debs was speaking to him personally. It was as if the two of them were

The Red Special

having a friendly chat. When Debs told his hearers that society could be transformed if only they would unite to do it, they were themselves transformed. Dozens of people followed him to his hotel room. They wanted to shake his hand. They wanted to tell him that by God he was right.

William Howard Taft was running on the Republican ticket; William Jennings Bryan headed the Democrats. Both were alarmed as they read about the crowds Eugene was drawing. In their speeches they aimed blow after blow at the socialists.

Meanwhile Eugene's campaign manager was struck with an amazing idea. Let the Party rent a locomotive, a sleeping car, and a baggage car. Let the little train be loaded with socialist "literature," and let Eugene Debs ride across the country and speak. The "Red Special" could start from Chicago, go down to southern California, then up the coast to the state of Washington, and from there come back to Chicago.

It sounded fantastic. But the Party was soon convinced that it could be done. Why, it wouldn't cost more than $20,000 to rent the train. And the money could be raised by contributions.

On August 30, Debs boarded the Red Special.

Eugene's brother Theodore was with him. So was Eugene's special Terre Haute friend, Stephen Reynolds, who had just written a biography of Debs. Thousands of copies, with a rising red sun on the cover, were aboard the Special along with stacks of other books and pamphlets and cartons of red socialist buttons. Every person on board was a socialist, including Harry Parker, who had charge of the train.

The details had all been worked out. In each state the local

Party leaders would be picked up and would introduce Debs to their home communities. There would be long stops in the important cities and shorter stops in between.

It was a campaign unheard of. As the little train moved through the prairies, friendly engineers blew their locomotive whistles. In Omaha, Nebraska, the local socialists decorated the Special with red streamers, which floated from the roof and wheels and rear platform. Farmers traveled miles in their buggies just to see the Red Special pass. At times crowds forced the little train to stop. Debs didn't mind. While he talked to the farmers from the rear platform, Theodore and Reynolds went around selling "literature." Five thousand people came to hear Eugene in Denver. Two thousand stood in the street while he spoke in Leadville. In California the crowds were bigger still. Debs never let them down. He had the answers.

Once a heckler called out: "Anybody that votes for the Socialists is just throwing his vote away!"

Debs came back at him instantly: "You argue that you are throwing your vote away. That's right. Don't vote for freedom —you might not get it. Vote for slavery—you have a cinch on that."

Eugene was never flustered, never at a loss. Many a listener went away from a meeting saying, "By God, he's right!" Debs was carrying on an educational campaign such as the country had never seen.

Gompers was supporting Bryan. Debs thought that was bad enough, but it was unforgivable to say that the Republicans were paying for the Red Special when Gompers knew very well that it was mainly the nickels and dimes of poor men and women that

Campaigning from "THE RED SPECIAL," 1908

The Red Special

were paying for the train. As for himself, Debs was getting $3 a day. Out of this he had to pay for meals and other expenses. Let Gompers make the most of that!

But the really important thing was how long Eugene could keep up the pace. In two weeks he made 130 speeches. He kept going on nerve, for his body refused to take the abuse he gave it. Sometimes he would crawl out of bed to make a speech, then crawl right in again. He drove himself. He told himself he had to. If he didn't, who would tell these people about socialism? He had a priceless message, and they thirsted to hear it.

Theodore was anxious. "If we don't give him a chance to rest," he told Reynolds, "Gene will never finish the trip."

The two worked out a scheme. At night, when at some station a crowd began to shout for Debs, Theodore, who greatly resembled his brother, would step out on the rear platform. With his collar turned up and hat brim pulled down, he passed for Eugene.

Then Reynolds would announce: "Comrade Debs is quite tired. We are now behind schedule. We have a very important meeting in the next town. Comrade Debs will not speak."

Theodore would then quickly step back into the car and the two conspirators would shake hands. They had got away with it again!

After a few days of this, Eugene was again able to address a crowd. And people came in the thousands. By September 25, when the Red Special got back to Chicago after traveling 9,000 miles, no less than 275,000 people had heard the Socialist candidate for president. Not one of them would ever forget Debs. He gave his listeners hope. He restored their dignity, he made them feel they were men. Employers spoke of workers as hands—mill

81

hands, factory hands, machine hands. Was the employer the only one what had a head? No, by God!

New York was the high point. The ten thousand seats at the Hippodrome had been sold out four days before. The audience went wild when Debs stepped out on the stage. For twenty-five minutes they cheered. They laughed and cried and waved red flags. They were demonstrating not only to welcome Eugene Debs. They were crying out against the system that oppressed them.

Eugene gave them one of the best speeches he had ever made:

"The historic mission of this movement," he said, "is to abolish capitalism and organize society upon a basis of collective ownership. This change is coming just as certain as I stand in your presence. It will come as soon as you are ready for it, and you will be ready for it just as soon as you understand what socialism means. . . .

"You read in the newspapers that under socialism you will be reduced to the dead level of degradation. You are there now. They tell you that socialism will destroy your individuality. You haven't got any. What is individuality? It is the human being in full bloom. The thirty million wage workers who are dependent upon the capitalist system for work are walking apologies, most of them. They have hinges in their knees. They doff their hats in the presence of a two-by-four boss. They have to beg to live, and they have no individuality."

Socialism, Debs told the huge audience, would bring an end to war. It would be the beginning of a reign of peace on earth and good will toward all men. Under socialism people would live happily together, enjoying the fruits of their labor. And in that happy hour the only badge of nobility would be the badge of labor.

The *New York Times* called it the greatest political meeting ever held in the city.

Next day Debs went to address the workers in the tenement district. As the truck plowed its way through a roaring ocean of people, the novelist Ernest Poole stood near Debs. Afterward he described the scene:

"No loud speakers, no brass bands. The truck stopped and Debs leaned out with both arms raised, smiling over the roaring crowd. Stillness came. And then only his voice was heard—a voice that could do with a crowd what it willed, not because of the mind behind it but because of the great warm heart which the crowd felt speaking there."

Philadelphia, Camden, Pittsburgh, Cincinnati, Evansville. In Woodstock five hundred people heard Debs speak from the steps of the jail where he had spent six months. Eugene called the jail the *college* in which he had been educated.

Back in Chicago, Debs and Bill Haywood marched in a parade for two miles at the head of 14,000 workers. Sixteen thousand people listened while Eugene Debs gave the last speech of the campaign in the Seventh Regiment Armory.

The *St. Louis Mirror* made a prediction: Debs would get one and a half million votes.

Eugene was near collapse by the time he got back to Terre Haute. Gratefully he dropped into his bed and let Kate nurse him. Together with Theodore, they waited for the votes to be counted.

After all that effort, after all those crowds, after all the enthusiasm, the results were disappointing. The socialists got no more than 420,710 votes, about the same as in 1904.

Had the votes been miscounted? Purposely?

Debs would not pursue it. Notwithstanding the campaign results, his hopes for the Party were high. "It is entirely possible," he let himself think, "that in four years more the Socialist party may sweep the nation."

13

To Keep His Country Out of War

In November of the election year 1912, Eugene was fifty-seven years old. He had been his party's presidential candidate for the fourth time and had polled 897,000 votes.

"Why so few?" he wondered, noting at the same time that the number was twice what it had been four years before. He had spoken five and six times a day. He had made speeches sixty-eight days in a row. He had put his heart into every speech. He had all but killed himself.

"It's the newspapers," Debs concluded. "They confuse and deceive the people."

He was still writing for the *Appeal to Reason*, but now Julius Wayland was dead and the paper wasn't the same. Eugene decided to quit. Kate wanted him to stay home, he said. He thought he would retire.

He had no idea that the most important part of his life still lay ahead, that his socialist convictions were to be tested in fierce fire, and that his courage was to be tried as it had never been tried before.

Already the stage was being set. There were rumblings of war in Europe.

Long ago an Englishman had told the British king that the quickest way for a country to get rich was to take riches away from some other country. England had become a great empire by doing just that. Both Russia and France had likewise been adding to their domains. As for Germany, fifty years had not passed since she had fought a war with France and had taken away the provinces of Alsace and Lorraine. There was bitter feeling in France about that. In fact, the pot was boiling all over Europe. Since no country would peaceably give up anything it had gained, Europe was preparing for war. Indeed, war seemed so near that the national committee of the Socialist party in the United States put out a statement saying that socialists were opposed to war—to this war and all wars.

Debs had thought of retiring. But after two months in Terre Haute had quietly gone by, he became restless. The foremost woman socialist in the country, Kate O'Hare, was lecturing and writing for the *National Rip-Saw*. Her husband Frank was its editor. Frank had worked with Debs on the Moyer-Haywood defense, and both husband and wife were close friends of Eugene's. When he was offered a job lecturing and writing for the *Rip-Saw*, he eagerly accepted and went on the road.

86

Antiwar button, about 1917

To Keep His Country Out of War

He was well aware of the rumblings in Europe. Yet what affected him most were matters that more immediately concerned Americans. He pointed out that marines were being sent to Mexico. What business did the president have to send armed men to Mexico? They were being sent there to protect the property of Standard Oil!

The Mexican flurry over, Debs turned his attention to Rockefeller's coalfields in Colorado, where miners were waging a strike. The Governor had sent in militia to escort strikebreakers through the picket line set up by the miners. In protest, the strikers left the town and put up tents in a nearby meadow. The militia turned machine guns on the strikers and then burned down the tents. Eleven children and two women were burnt to death.

The whole country rang with horrified protest. But far from being restrained by the outcry, President Wilson sent federal troops to crush the strike.

That same month of August 1914, war broke out in Europe.

Debs was no scholar. He had forgotten the French and German his father had taught him and could read no language but English. An ocean three thousand miles wide separated him from what was happening in Europe. But socialism taught him what the fighting was all about. It was a commercial and industrial war. It was the result of fifty years of competition among the capitalist nations. In each country the masters were after the same thing: to rule over more land and people, to have greater power to rob, and to increase their ill-gotten wealth.

What did the American people have to do with such a war? Debs asked. The answer was NOTHING. Therefore let the United States remain neutral. America should stay out of the war.

87

And what was a socialist's duty in this heart-breaking time when rivers of blood were pouring out in Europe? A socialist's duty, Eugene told himself, was to speak out for peace. It was to explain the causes of the war. It was to get people to understand something about the social system in which they lived. A socialist's duty was to appeal to the reason and conscience of all people and prepare them to change their country—by perfectly peaceable and orderly means—into a real democracy.

Come what might, he would stand firm, Debs decided. He would be a true socialist in word and deed. It saddened him to reflect on how the European socialists had behaved. Only a tiny handful had had the courage to stand up for socialist principles. When the test came, nearly all had become "patriots." They had declared their nation to be right and the enemy wrong. As if there could be any right, any honor among thieves! As if the working class of all countries was not equally oppressed. Only a few remembered the slogan: "Workingmen of all countries, unite!"

Well, he had his work cut out for him. Whatever happened to him in the difficult time ahead, he would be true to himself. He would do all he could to keep his country out of the war.

14

Teetering on the Edge

Touring the Midwest, Texas, and the West Coast, Debs felt the sudden change that had come over the country. For the past two years the United States had been sunk in a depression. Now, as a flood of war orders poured in from the Allies, factories once more began to hum. A mighty call sounded for hands to turn out guns, bullets, explosives, munitions of all sorts.

Eugene talked peace. Week after week he wrote about peace. But what effect could one man have on the American masses in the face of the daily pounding of the newspapers? They said Germany had to be defeated. They said the United States must not let the Allies down. They said the nation must do all it could to help them—short of sending American boys over to fight. President Wilson had promised to keep America out of the war. In 1915 came the first Allied War Loan. President Wilson might *say* he was keeping America out of the war, but the war loan was a big step toward taking the United States into it. Steadily, day by day and month by month, the country was drifting closer to the edge. *Preparedness* now became the most popular word in the language.

Even socialists were for preparedness. There was danger, some of them said, of our being invaded by Germany. The socialist writer Upton Sinclair held that Germany must be defeated at all costs. He had written a statement and sent a copy to Debs.

Eugene would not sign it. He remembered too well the massacre in Colorado. Neither Germans nor any other foreign enemy could do worse to labor than "the Rockefellers and their pirate pals" were doing.

With a shiver of disgust Debs watched prominent socialists abandon their principles and become *patriots*. And wasn't it right for patriots to be prepared? Every socialist who changed horses was convinced he had good reason.

But Debs would not compromise. When he was asked where he stood, he answered: "I am opposed to every war but one; I am for that war with heart and soul, and that is the worldwide war of the social revolution. In that war I am prepared to fight in any way the ruling class may make necessary, even to the barricades. That is where I stand, and where I believe the Socialist party stands, or ought to stand, on the question of war."

Some in the Party didn't approve of what Debs said. In particular they didn't like what he wrote in the spring of 1916 when President Wilson sent American troops to chase the Mexican

90

rebel, Pancho Villa. To Debs this was just another case of the government coming out on the side of the corporations.

"I want the people of America to understand," he wrote, "that if we have war with Mexico, our boys will not be fighting for their country. They'll be fighting for the Wall Street interests that own four billion dollars' worth of property in Mexico for which they paid not one hundredth part. That's all there is to this Mexican trouble."

No, some in the Socialist party didn't like that open statement by Debs. Eugene Debs might be a very good speaker and writer, but he was giving the socialists a bad name. It would be better not to run him for president in the 1916 campaign.

Allen L. Benson, a journalist, was chosen to run instead.

Eugene was relieved. He didn't want to run for president. Four times was enough.

But what could he do when the socialists in Terre Haute nominated him for Congress? He tried to get out of it by saying he wasn't well. They wouldn't accept that. Hadn't he sworn time and again that he would serve the Party and carry out any task it assigned to him? He had to accept.

It meant campaigning, and Debs campaigned. He was an old hand at it. He got into a Model T Ford and went out on the Indiana roads. When he got to a town, he drove up to the square, climbed out of the car, and gave his speech. As the crowd grew, he would clamber up on the hood and keep on talking. He talked peace. He spoke against munition makers—and never had he spoken with more passion. He talked as if the fate of the world depended on himself alone. He *must* keep America out of the war. He must show people what this capitalist war—*any* capitalist war—was

91

about. In the first two weeks on the road he made fifty-five speeches.

People were enthusiastic. But the enthusiasm didn't last. There was the everlasting pounding of the newspapers. There was the constant propaganda from the other side.

When the campaign was over, Debs went back to Terre Haute. There was a parade, and he and Kate marched at the head of it. Then came the voting and the counting of ballots. Debs had the satisfaction of knowing that he got more than three times as many votes as the socialist candidate from the Fifth District of Indiana had won in the last election. But the Republicans won. As for the socialist nominee for president, he polled three hundred thousand fewer votes than Debs got in 1912.

The country was rushing toward war. Could anything stop it?

It took great courage to be independent in the midst of the crowd. In France Jean Jaurés, the leader of the antiwar socialists, was assassinated. In England and Germany the antiwar socialists were in prison. The Russian socialists had been marched off to Siberia. Debs wondered how long it would be before he, too, was in prison.

In that winter of 1916 signs of the new prosperity were everywhere. The munitions plants were going full blast and skilled workers were getting high wages. Wheat and cotton had risen sky-high, farmers were getting better prices for what they raised, while corporation profits were soaring. Nobody seemed worried about neutrality. People felt safe. Hadn't Wilson said he would keep America out of the war?

All the time the United States was teetering on the edge. It needed only an announcement from Germany to send the country

Teetering on the Edge

plunging. When, on the first of February 1917, Germany said that her submarines would attack all shipping, no matter whose, President Wilson broke off relations. The next step would be war. It hadn't yet been declared, but its shadow hung over the nation.

Eugene was in bed with the flu when the German ambassador sailed home. But in March he was touring the eastern states. He doubted he could change the direction in which the country was moving, but at least he would talk peace until they stopped him.

Wilson asked for national unity. There was a lot in the papers about standing by the president. To Debs it was clear that his audiences didn't know where they stood and were very uneasy about being undecided. They wanted Debs to tell them where *he* stood so they could make up their minds.

"I am willing to stand by the president," Debs told them, "if he stands for the things I want. But when I look at the gang that stands behind the president, I know it isn't my crowd."

Then he repeated what he had often said: "This is a war for profits. What interest can workingmen have in such a war?"

In New York City two thousand people filled the hall in which Debs was to speak, while another two thousand milled about the doors but couldn't get in. New York was the city of Wall Street and the stock market. This was the headquarters of *preparedness*. But the faces he saw looking up at him were the lined, worried faces of workingmen and workingwomen. What should he say to these people who had nothing to gain from capitalist war?

"If Congress declares war," Debs told them, "workingmen should join a general strike!"

Even as he said it, Eugene knew that he was recommending the impossible. There wasn't one chance in a thousand that labor, led by such men as Gompers, would declare itself in favor of a general strike. Labor had been bought by high wages. It had been misled by the newspapers. It was prepared to be putty in the hands of the warmakers.

Six days after Debs proposed the idea of a general strike, the AFL and the railway brotherhoods promised that if the United States were drawn into the war, they would offer their services to their country. More. They would call upon their fellow workers and fellow citizens to do the same.

On April 6, 1917, the United States declared war.

15

Let the Government Do Its Worst

Eugene Debs had done all one man could to keep the United States out of the war. He was heartsick. What now?

Gloomily he sat at home in Terre Haute, thinking it over, trying to decide what his next step should be. Above his desk hung a picture of Karl Marx. He looked earnestly at it, and as he looked it seemed to him that the face became that of Victor Hugo. "Yes," he thought, "people *can* be redeemed by brotherhood." He believed it, believed it! But how could he go out and talk to people about brotherhood now?

The telephone rang. It was Charles Ruthenberg calling to say that the Socialist party was holding a convention in St. Louis. The

Party was about to state is position on the war and wanted him there to help.

"Haven't I already made my position on the war perfectly clear?" Debs asked. He would not go. It was up to the delegates to decide where the Party stood.

To his immense satisfaction, the Party came through. Five days after the United States declared war, a majority of the delegates stated that they stood by the working class. They were against the war just declared by the United States.

That war was not caused, the statement said, by accident. Nor had it been brought about by any *one* country. It was the result of capitalist competition. The United States had been pressured into the war by greedy American capitalists who wanted still greater profits. They were not satisfied with the seven billion dollars they had already made from the manufacture and sale of munitions and war supplies and from the export of food and other necessities.

"We brand the declaration of war by our government," the socialists said, "as a crime against the people of the United States and against the nations of the world."

The Party had come through. Yet Debs knew that it was weaker than its statement. That statement had been adopted by most of the rank and file socialists. But now that war had been declared, Debs was afraid that many important people would leave the Socialist party. And the trade unions would line up behind Gompers. Hadn't they said they were ready to serve the government in every way?

There was another weakness which Debs was shortly to discover. The socialist magazines and papers were disappearing. One by one as their second class mailing privileges were taken

96

away, they folded. Some changed their name and watched their step. Even the *Appeal to Reason* did that—it went along with the policies of Woodrow Wilson.

Debs thought it amazing that in the spring of 1917 there was still so much opposition to the war. For three years, newspapers, preachers, and college professors had called "Preparedness! Preparedness!" And still many thousands were openly against the war and the draft. He hoped he had had something to do with it. Not everyone was singing "America, Here's My Boy!"

Washington took anxious note. "The government cannot carry on war if there is open dissent!" congressmen declared.

Congress passed the Espionage Act. The First Amendment to the Constitution forbade Congress to make any law abridging free speech or the freedom of the press, but what of that? Wasn't the United States at WAR? Not only did Congress pass the Espionage Act. The authorities stretched its meaning to cover anyone who by word or deed interfered with the conduct of the war.

Arrest after arrest was made. This one was charged with obstructing the draft, that one with making an antiwar speech. "Patriotic" people took the law into their own hands. They fell upon socialists and pacificists. They tarred and feathered IWW men. In Bisbee, Arizona, a vigilance committee herded 1,162 IWW men into cattle cars, shipped them out into the desert, and left them there without food or water. "Patriots" burned German books in the street. They forced professors suspected of being pro-German to leave their jobs. Right in Debs's own Terre Haute, Theodore's neighbor, a grocer of German parentage, was beaten up by a banker while an obliging policeman held the grocer's arms. For what? For saying something that sounded "unpatriotic" to the sensitive ears of the banker. A socialist coal digger in a mining camp outside the town was all but lynched for refusing to buy a Liberty Bond. People bought Liberty Bonds in self-defense. If they didn't, they were suspect.

Eugene wrote protests in *Social Revolution*—that was the new name of the *Rip-Saw*—but he was careful not to antagonize.

News of the revolution in Russia sent a flood of hope surging through Eugene. The first socialist government in the world! And those workers and peasants knew what they were doing! They had seized power and had asked for an international peace conference. When their appeal was rejected, they took their country out of the war. How Debs hoped the ideas of the Bolsheviks would come to prevail in his own country!

But the very thing that made Debs rejoice alarmed the United States government. A wave of arrests, raids, and indictments followed the Russian Revolution. It was said that a thousand people were indicted and that two hundred of them were convicted. The Espionage Act was serving the government well.

As Debs had foreseen, many of those who had adopted the Socialist party's manifesto found the going too hard for them. They had *said* they believed the war was the result of capitalist competition. They had called President Wilson a "tool of Wall Street." Now they called him the "champion of democracy."

Clearly these socialists were falling by the wayside. They were going the way of the European socialists who stood by their own war-makers. It was sad, sad, Eugene thought. But he himself could not act. The horror in Europe paralyzed him. All the fire had gone out of his writing.

Then suddenly he came to life. Once more he could fight.

98

Let the Government Do Its Worst

Perhaps what woke him up more than anything else was that Kate O'Hare had been convicted for speaking against the war. He could not believe that this magnificent person would be sent to prison just for exercising her right of free speech. If they sent Kate O'Hare to prison, he would feel guilty to be free!

He began to organize a defense campaign for her and other political prisoners.

The hypocrisy of the president! He was forever talking about democracy, democracy. And here were Kate O'Hare and others being sent to prison for exercising their constitutional rights. What kind of democracy was that? The time had come for him to speak out against the war and accept the consequences. They'd nail him, but that was all right.

Yes, it would be all right. Let the government do its worst. He wanted to arouse people to oppose the war, but even more he wanted to turn the government's attention to himself. Let it place him on trial. He would either open the prison doors for Kate O'Hare and the rest of the comrades or he would close them on himself. He had not been joking when he said that if Kate O'Hare went to prison, he felt guilty to be free.

He went on a speaking tour. In Indiana and Illinois he spoke a dozen times against the war. The government paid no attention. Oh, how good it was to be again on the offensive! If only the government would turn its eyes on him! Perhaps in Ohio it would be different. Ohio had convicted three Cleveland socialists for opposing the draft act. Charles Ruthenberg, who had pleaded with him to come to the socialist convention, and two other comrades were now in the workhouse in Canton, Ohio.

On June 16, 1918, Eugene was in Canton to speak to the Ohio

convention of the Socialist party. The workhouse was almost across the street from the park where he was to speak. He decided to pay the three socialists a visit first. He wanted them to know that he respected their courage and that, like them, he was about to confront the government.

16

Yours But to Do and Die

It was a hot Sunday afternoon that June 16. A crowd of some 1,200 people—mostly working people—had gathered at Nimsimilla Park and were impatiently waiting to hear Eugene Debs. As the man who had been four times candidate for president stepped to the front of the wooden bandstand, the audience burst into welcoming applause.

A great love swelled Eugene's heart. He stretched out his arms as though to embrace these brothers and sisters of his. And stillness succeeded the clapping.

It had always been a high privilege to him, Debs said, to speak for labor, to plead the cause of the men and women and children who toiled. He had just returned from a visit over yonder—he pointed toward the workhouse—where three of their most loyal comrades were imprisoned.

"They have come to realize," Debs said, "as many of us have, that it is extremely dangerous to exercise the constitutional right of free speech in a country fighting to make democracy safe in the world."

He realized, he said, that he must be exceedingly careful, prudent as to what he said, and even more careful and prudent as to how he said it. He might not be able to say all that he thought. But he was not going to say anything he did not think. He would a thousand times rather be a free soul in jail than a coward in the streets.

With that, Debs cast prudence to the winds.

There were many, he said, who sought refuge in the popular side of a great question. As a socialist, he had long learned to stand alone. The capitalist newspapers had been saying that he had suddenly come to his senses, that he had stopped being a wicked socialist and had become a patriotic socialist. As if he had ever been anything else! What was this deliberate misrepresentation for? The purpose was to make it appear that the socialists were divided, that they were pitted against each other. But socialists were not born yesterday. They knew how to read capitalist newspapers and to believe exactly the opposite of what they read.

Debs brought up the revolution in Russia. "Why," he asked, "should a socialist be discouraged on the eve of the greatest triumph in all the history of the socialist movement?"

He spoke of those who had the moral courage to stand by their convictions, to fight for them, go to jail or to hell for them. "They

102

Debs making an antiwar speech on June 16, 1918, Canton, Ohio

are writing their names in fadeless letters in the history of mankind,'' said Debs. ''Those boys over yonder,'' and again he indicated the workhouse, ''are my younger brothers. Their lips, though temporarily mute, are more eloquent than ever before; and their voice, though silent, is heard around the world. . . .

''Are we opposed to Prussian militarism? Why, we have been fighting it since the day the socialist movement was born. And we are going to continue to fight it, day and night, until it is wiped from the face of the earth.''

Thunderous applause approved this statement.

Debs waited till the clapping and the cheers died down. Then he reminded his hearers of some bits of history: how Theodore Roosevelt had hobnobbed with the Kaiser; how the brother of Emperor William—the ''Beast of Berlin''—had been wined and dined by wealthy Americans. He ridiculed the Wall Street junkers who bought the titles of broken-down princes, dukes, and counts for their daughters.

''These are the gentry who are today wrapped up in the American flag,'' said Debs, ''who shout their claim from the housetops that they are the only patriots.''

He spoke of Tom Mooney, labor leader, his good friend, imprisoned for life because of a crime he didn't commit. ''If he ought to go to the gallows, so ought I,'' said Debs. ''If he is guilty, every man who belongs to a labor organization or to the Socialist party is likewise guilty.''

He talked about Kate O'Hare who had been sentenced to the penitentiary for five years simply for exercising the right of free speech.

Then he asked: Who appointed the federal judges? The people? Never. And when those judges went on the bench, they did not go to serve the people but to serve the interest that placed them and kept them where they were.

"Why, the other day," said Debs, "by a vote of five to four—a kind of craps game: 'come seven, come 'leven'—they declared the child labor law unconstitutional." They had wiped that law from the statute books "so that we may continue to grind the flesh and blood and bones of puny little children into profits for the junkers of Wall Street." And this in a country that boasts of fighting to make the world safe for democracy!

"Our hearts," Debs said, "are with the Bolsheviki of Russia. These Russian comrades of ours have made greater sacrifices, have suffered more, and have shed more heroic blood than any like number of men and women anywhere on earth. And the very first act of the triumphant Russian Revolution was to proclaim a state of peace with all mankind."

He told his audience that they had called upon all nations to send representatives to a conference to lay down terms of a peace that should be just and lasting. "Here was the supreme opportunity to make the world safe for democracy."

Was there any response? "No, not the slightest attention was paid to it by the Christian nations organized in the terrible slaughter."

Throughout history, Debs said, wars had been waged for conquest and plunder. The master class had always declared the wars; the subject class had always fought the battles. The master class had all to gain and nothing to lose, while the subject class had nothing to gain and all to lose—especially their lives.

104

Yours But to Do and Die

And Debs added sarcastically:

Yours not to reason why;
Yours but to do and die.

He let the lines sink in. Then he said:

"You need at this time especially to know that you are fit for something better than slavery and cannon fodder. You need to know that you have a mind to improve, a soul to develop, and a manhood to sustain. You need to know that as long as you are ignorant, as long as you are indifferent, as long as you are unorganized, you will be degraded, and you will have to beg for a job. You will get just enough for your slavish toil to keep you in working order."

Capitalists, said Debs, gave themselves credit for having superior brains. It was this, they claimed, that put their class on top. "They are continually talking about your patriotic duty," Debs went on. "It is not *their* but *your* patriotic duty that they are concerned about. There is a decided difference. Their patriotic duty never takes them to the firing line or chucks them into the trenches. . . .

"Yes, a change is certainly needed, not merely a change of party, but a change of system, a change from slavery to freedom. When this change comes at last, we shall rise from brutehood to brotherhood. And to accomplish it we have to educate and organize workers industrially and politically. All of you workers in a given industry should belong to one and the same union.

"When you have organized industrially, you will soon learn that you can manage as well as operate industry. You will soon

105

realize that you do not need the idle masters and employers. They are simply parasites. They do not employ you as you imagine, but you employ them to take from you what you produce. You do not need them to depend upon for your jobs. You must own your own tools and then you will control your own jobs, enjoy the products of your own labor, and be free men instead of industrial slaves . . .

"Yes, in good time we are going to sweep into power in this nation and throughout the world. The sun of capitalism is setting; the sun of socialism is rising. We socialists are the builders of the beautiful world that is to be. We are inviting—aye challenging— you this afternoon in the name of your own manhood and woman- hood to join us and do your part.

"In due time the hour will strike, and this cause triumphant—the greatest in history—will proclaim the emancipa- tion of the working class and the brotherhood of mankind."

17

In the Toils of the Law

Debs had talked for two hours, and, as usual, the audience had hung on his words. So had a government stenographer. All the time Eugene was talking, the stenographer had been taking down the speech word for word.

Scattered among the crowd had been a number of men of draft age. They had not been allowed to listen undisturbed—perhaps some were here who ought by rights to be in the trenches! A touch on the shoulder and a "Let's see your draft card, Buddy!" had set the young men resentfully digging in their pockets. The law! Theirs not to reason why, theirs but to do and die!

After the Canton speech, Eugene kept on with his Ohio tour, kept on serving the Cause, talking peace. He vividly remembered the Civil War and how he had watched the trains carrying men and boys away. He remembered wondering what was "glory."

A fine word *glory*. It often appeared in the "patriotic" speeches reported in the newspapers. But what exactly was *glory?* Certainly it was not to be found in the trenches. . .

Two weeks passed. Eugene was about to make a speech at a socialist picnic in Cleveland when the law caught up with him. He was charged with violating the Espionage Law at Canton, Ohio. He had had a hunch that that speech would settle matters for him, though he had said no more than he had said many times before.

It was a Sunday. Debs was unable to arrange for bond and spent the night in a cell. But next morning when friends put up a bond for him, he was free again—free until the trial. That was set for the ninth of September.

There wasn't much chance of his being free after the ninth, he thought, so he refused to run for Congress. Instead he would support the socialist candidate.

As late as Labor Day he was speaking for peace. Even on the fifth of September he was urging a strong campaign to free political prisoners: Kate O'Hare was in a Missouri prison.

It was time now to prepare his own defense. Eugene chose four of the best socialist lawyers available and talked things over with them.

Actually there was almost nothing for the lawyers to do. It was quickly agreed that they would admit Eugene had made the speech. But they would deny that his speech was a crime. Their argument would be that the Espionage Act was unconstitutional.

Eugene had no hope of being acquitted, but he meant to put up

108

In the Toils of the Law

a fight. He knew he would have a chance to confront the jury and meant to make the most of the opportunity. He was for peace. He was also for free speech. His voice would be heard far beyond the courtroom. Before the government silenced him—perhaps for the rest of his life—he would stand up for free speech. . . .

There was a flurry of excitement as Eugene, with one his counsel, came into the crowded courtroom. The lawyers had urged that Kate Debs be present. They didn't want the jury to think of Eugene as some sort of inhuman creature but as a man like themselves, a man with a wife. However, every time they mentioned it, Debs had been against having Kate there. It would not be good for her health, he said.

Head high, Eugene took his seat at a table and folded his hands in his lap. Clearly he was eager to take part in the scene that was to be the high point of his life.

He glanced at the jury—twelve well-to-do, respectable citizens, their average age in the seventies. They didn't look as if they would be sympathetic.

He glanced at Judge Westenhaver sitting behind his imposing table. The judge looked grim.

Nor could the prosecutor be expected to be anything but harsh. Eugene heard himself described as ''the palpitating pulse of the sedition crusade.''

It was a relief to the audience to hear lawyer Seymour Stedman give a different character to their hero. Stedman traced Debs's career. Then he said to the jury: ''We ask you to judge Eugene V. Debs by his life, his deeds, and his works. If you will do that, we shall abide by your verdict.''

109

Clapping broke out in the audience. But the judge would have none of it.

"Arrest that man and that woman!" he shouted. "Arrest everybody you saw clapping their hands!"

One of Eugene's lawyers tried to restrain the angry judge. "I don't like to see you sit there and play God to your fellow men," the lawyer said.

The remark was so unexpected that the judge was startled into adjourning court for the day. . . .

During the two days that followed, the government brought out its witnesses. The stenographer read the Canton speech. Others told how many people had been in the park and that men of draft age were among the listeners. When the last witness had given his evidence, the prosecutor closed the government's case.

"Let's see—you rest," Stedman said. "We rest."

The audience gasped. What? Would no defense be made for Eugene Debs? What did it mean?

The judge declared a ten-minute recess. But the audience did not move. They were afraid of losing their seats. The corridors were crowded with Eugene's friends, who had been standing in line for hours in the hope of getting in to watch the trial.

When at two o'clock the court reconvened, Stedman made an announcement that sent a thrill through the courtroom. Eugene Debs would make his own plea to the jury.

Slowly Debs walked to the jury box. In one hand he carried some papers. The entire audience, the judge, the jury, the prosecutor, watched as if for lightning while for a full minute Debs looked into the faces of his judges. At last he spoke.

In the Toils of the Law

He wished to admit the truth of all that had been testified, he said. But he would not take back a word—not even to save himself from going to the penitentiary for the rest of his days.

The jury, Debs said, had heard the report of his speech. There was not a word there to warrant the charges. His purpose had been simply to make the people understand something about the social system in which they lived. His purpose had been to prepare them to change that system by peaceable means into a real democracy.

It was not true that he believed in force and violence as the prosecution had said. He had never advocated violence in any form. He had always believed in education and enlightenment. He had made his appeal to the reason and conscience of the people. He was doing the little he could to bring about a change that should do away with the rule of the great body of the people by a relatively small class and establish in this country an industrial and social democracy. Those who attacked the established order of things had always had to pay a penalty.

Yet when a great change occurred in history, the majority as a rule was wrong, Debs told the jury. The minority was usually right. Washington, Ben Franklin, and Tom Paine were the minority leaders of their day. The Tories had called them criminals. The abolitionists, those brave men and women who opposed chattel slavery, had been the despised minority.

He had criticized and condemned the war, Debs said, because he believed it was his duty to do so. Abraham Lincoln, Charles Sumner, Daniel Webster, and Henry Clay had all denounced the Mexican War and called it a crime against humanity. They had not been charged with treason nor tried for crime. In 1864 the Demo-

111

cratic party had condemned the Civil War as a failure. Were the Democrats traitors? If so, why were they not indicted and prosecuted?

"I believe in the Constitution," said Debs. And he read aloud the First Amendment.

"I believe the revolutionary fathers meant what is here stated. That is the right I exercised at Canton. And for the exercise of that right, I now have to answer to this indictment.

"Gentlemen of the jury, I cannot take back a word I have said. I cannot repudiate a sentence I have uttered. I stand before you guilty of having made this speech. I do not know, I cannot tell, what your verdict may be. Nor does it matter much, so far as I am concerned.

"Gentlemen, I am the smallest part of this trial. There is an infinitely greater issue that is being tried today in this court, though you may not be conscious of it. American institutions are on trial here before a court of American citizens. The future will render the verdict."

As Eugene slowly returned to his seat, several of the jurymen were seen to be crying.

When Eugene and his lawyers were planning the defense, all had agreed that Debs was sure to be convicted. Their belief was prophetic. Though some of the jury had been moved to tears, their verdict was nevertheless: "Guilty as charged in the indictment." In their opinion Debs had willfully and knowingly tried to obstruct the operation of the conscription act.

How many years would the judge give him? That was the next important question.

His lawyers wanted Debs to make another speech: it was his

right to do so before being sentenced. But he absolutely refused to try to soften the judge. Eugene seemed not to care if he died in prison.

The lawyers loved their client and kept insisting that he speak again. In the end Debs gave in. All right. He would say a few words more.

When court opened on Saturday September 13 and the clerk asked if the defendant would like to make a final statement, Debs got up. As if it was not he but someone else who was involved, he moved toward the judge's bench. Years later, when most people only vaguely remembered that Eugene had been a socialist who went to prison for opposing the First World War, there would be some who remembered his words in that stilled courtroom:

"Your Honor, years ago I recognized my kinship with all living things and I made up my mind that I was not one bit better than the meanest of the earth. I said then, I say now, that while there is a lower class, I am in it; while there is a criminal element, I am of it; while there is a soul in prison, I am not free. . . .

"I am thinking this morning of the men in the mills and factories; I am thinking of the women who, for a paltry wage, are compelled to work out their lives; of the little children who, in this system, are robbed of their childhood becaused money is still so much more important than human life. Gold is God and rules in the affairs of men. . . .

"I can see the dawn of a better day of humanity. The people are awakening. In due course of time they will come into their own."

When Debs finished speaking, Judge Westerhaven sat unmoved. He sat in his high seat looking as grim and righteous as when the trial opened. It seemed to him that the old man before him deluded himself into thinking that he served humanity and the downtrodden. The judge was himself a lover of peace, he said. He was himself a defender of the Constitution of the United States.

Doubtless he thought he was being humane and merciful when he sentenced the defendant to ten years in prison.

18

Walls and Bars

Eugene's lawyers didn't let the matter rest there; they appealed to the Supreme Court. Let it say whether the Espionage Act was constitutional.

Free on bail, Eugene went home to Terre Haute. He had insisted that the Supreme Court was just an arm of capitalism and was bound to stand by the war-makers. He was therefore not surprised when on the tenth of March the Court upheld his conviction and sentence. Nor was he upset when a telephone call from District Attorney Wertz ordered him to make ready at once and come to Cleveland to surrender himself.

"Thank you, Mr. Wertz. I'll be right along," Eugene replied.

The war was over by this time. An armistice had been signed four months ago. Russia, of course, had long since signed a separate peace. But representatives of England, France, and Germany were at Versailles, wrangling over how much defeated Germany was to give up and to whom. Woodrow Wilson had gone to Versailles to help in the bargaining.

"Suppose President Wilson should cable a pardon for you, what would you do?" David Karsner, a young reporter on the *New York Call*, asked Debs. Karsner, who had reported the Cleveland trial, was spending the last day with Debs and was going with him to the prison door.

Eugene answered the question firmly. "I should refuse to accept it unless the same pardon were extended to every man and woman in prison under the Espionage Law. They must let them all out—or I won't come out."

That evening, while Eugene smoked a cigar and told jokes, the people he loved best in the world sat in the parlor with him, waiting for train time. Kate, Theodore, and his wife and daughter, Kate's mother Mrs. Baur, and the druggist Arthur Baur, Kate's brother, were all there. Arthur, who was also going with Debs as far as the prison, had a very special relationship with his brother-in-law. Eugene refused to set foot in a bank. Whenever he had money to deposit, Eugene would bring it to Arthur, and whenever he needed money, he would ask Arthur for it. Whether he had anything in the "bank" or not, Eugene always got more than he asked for.

"Well, Eugene, we had better start," Kate said. Nothing in her manner revealed what Eugene's going to prison meant to her. Kate was standing firm.

116

"Yes," Debs said, rising. "We don't want to miss the train."

Theodore got his brother's coat from the rack.

Old Mrs. Baur began to cry. "It's all right, mother," Eugene said as he patted her cheek tenderly. "It will come out all right in the end."

He had asked that there be no demonstration. Nevertheless more than two hundred workingmen and women were at the station to see him off. Debs went from one to another, expressing his love for each.

"By God," said a big miner, pushing through to Debs, "we're with you to the last man."

"I know it," said Eugene, patting his cheek and kissing his brow. "Until the last drop we'll stand together, all of us. You boys take care of the outside, and I'll take care of the inside."

"Hip-hip-hooray!" Cheers rang out again and again. But it was a joyless gathering. Nearly everyone there was silently wondering whether Gene would ever come back to Terre Haute.

Warden Joseph Terrell of the state prison at Moundsville, West Virginia, realized at once that Eugene Debs was a very special prisoner and allowed him unheard-of priviledges. Eugene could have as many visitors as he liked and write all the letters he wanted to. He could even receive socialist newspapers, provided he didn't pass them around. For work, the Warden gave him a light clerical job at the prison hospital.

Actually, however, Eugene was free most of the time to do what he liked, and the door to his cell was never locked. Later on he was even allowed to have the prison doctor's little house for his own.

As always, Eugene read a great deal. But he spent much of his time among the prisoners and soon became a sort of chaplain to them. He talked their problems over with the men, comforted them, wrote letters for them. He knew many of the prisoners by first name and felt at ease with them. Perhaps it was because his contact with the convicts was not so very different from his contact with workers. He saw deeply into men—any men—because he looked deep. And everywhere he looked, he saw the class struggle. Before long, Eugene came to regard the prisoners as victims of the social system, even as he himself was its victim. The prisoners had not seen the system for what it was, while he had seen it all too clearly.

"I belong in prison," Eugene told himself. "I belong where men are made to suffer for the wrongs committed against them by a brutalizing system."

A sense of brotherhood united him to the "inmates." Walls and bars seemed to give a deeper meaning to Eugene's vision of a society working for the benefit of all. At sixty-four the word *brotherhood* was even more precious to him than it had been that evening when at nineteen he joined the Brotherhood of Locomotive Firemen.

Eugene didn't check the days off on a calendar, and so two months passed almost without his realizing it. He was just beginning to understand the meaning of prison when one morning after breakfast Warden Terrell came in to his room and told him that orders had come from Washington. He was to be transferred to the

118

Walls and Bars

federal prison at Atlanta, Georgia, and he had one hour to pack.

"I'll be ready in a jiffy," Eugene said.

Quickly he gathered together the candy, fruit, and cigars his friends had sent him and went the rounds of the hospital, distributing gifts and saying good-bye to each man. A black trusty who loved Eugene helped him to pack.

Warden Terrell wanted to make it as easy as he could for Debs to transfer. In a letter to the warden at Atlanta, Terrell explained the kind of prisoner Eugene Debs was:

"I never in my life met a kinder man," Terrell wrote. "He is forever thinking of others, trying to serve them and never thinking of himself."

Notwithstanding, Warden Zerbst did not grant Debs the many privileges he had had at Moundsville. Like everyone else, Debs could write one letter a week to his family. He could have no papers or magazines. And he could receive only a "reasonable" number of visits from his family and friends. The warden offered Eugene a light clerical job at the hospital. But this he would not accept. It ended with his working from eight to four in the clothing warehouse and being treated like everyone else—as a common convict, as simply a number.

The first problem Eugene had to meet was food. On his lecture tours he was used to eating lumpy potatoes and meat cooked to death. But here food was so bad that two weeks passed before he could make himself eat at all. Nor did he have a private room. When he was not doing heavy labor in the warehouse, he was shut up for fifteen hours a day in a stifling cell with five other men. In two months time he lost twenty-five pounds and his health broke down so badly that Warden Zerbst was alarmed. He didn't want his most famous prisoner to die while in his keeping. He made Eugene clerk to the chief physician. In the hospital Debs could have slightly better food, sleep in a tiny room of his own on the top floor, and have a bed instead of a bunk. The change put Eugene on his feet, and soon he could go on with his painful study of prison life.

One of the first things that struck Eugene was that nearly all the prisoners were poor. Rich men, he reflected, did not as a rule go to prison. When one did go, he was an exception; he excited great curiosity and amazement. Debs was forced to conclude that *prisons were built for poor men*. Further, it became clearer and clearer to him that prisons could not be reformed. It was not enough to improve this or that aspect of prison life. Prisons must be done away with altogether. Crime sprang mainly from poverty, which bred misery. And misery bred crime. But it was society that created the poverty. Then it punished and degraded men for crime which poverty made them commit. Society punished because it thought the men were "bad."

But Eugene had never found a prisoner who was bad. He never found one who didn't respond to kindness, whether it was a word of advice or a pipeful of tobacco. This alone proved to Eugene that prisoners were not doomed to prison from the cradle due to being born with a natural bent for crime. The spiritless creatures he saw about him had once been ordinary men. Prison had killed their spirit. Long sentences had stripped them of their manhood. They cowered before the club of the keeper.

Eugene shuddered as he surveyed the cells. In each of them six sweating, suffering men were locked while armed guards

120

September, 1920.
Debs in prison in Atlanta, Georgia
during his fifth campaign for the Presidency.

watched that none should escape. It was clear to him that capitalism could never solve the problem of prisons and crime. Only socialism could build a society in which there was neither crime nor prison. "The time will surely come," he thought, "when man will think too well of himself to cage his brother as a brute, place an armed brute over him, feed him as a brute, treat him as a brute, and reduce him to the level of a brute."

Meantime the unfortunates whose life he shared were not aware that Eugene Debs was studying them. Nor did the guards. Yet Eugene was like leaven in a loaf of bread. To every prisoner he was soon known as "Little Jesus." Even the guards responded to his presence. . . .

In May 1920 a group of unexpected visitors came to Atlanta. They had been sent by the Socialist Party and they brought Eugene the news that he had been nominated for president.

Debs greeted the announcement with open joy.

"How will you conduct the campaign?" Seymour Stedman asked a bit anxiously.

Debs laughed. "I will be a candidate at home in seclusion," he answered. "My enemies will always know where to find me."

A man in prison candidate for president?!

Never had such a thing happened before. The nation was forced to take notice. And those who were working to get a general pardon for all political prisoners had another good argument in favor of amnesty.

At the moment the hopes of these people were high anyway. President Wilson, who had so long declared that the object of the World War was "to make the world safe for democracy," had now changed his mind. In September 1919 he had declared that the

121

World War was a commercial and industrial war. A lot of men and women were still in prison because they had said the same thing!

Eugene chafed because he could not reach the public. He thought of the crowds he had addressed in 1908 and 1912. He was relieved when, in the last months of this his fifth campaign, he was allowed to issue one bulletin a week to the United Press.

He used the privilege to attack Woodrow Wilson. Eugene bitterly hated the president. Debs couldn't see how this man could deny pardons to men and women who had gone to prison for saying the same thing he was now saying. It was not honest.

As the campaign went on, Eugene's health improved. The excitement was doing him good. Certainly it was good for the prisoners. Debs was *their* candidate. They were proud of him, they were happy for him. Many believed that Number 9653 would be the next president. "And then he'll pardon us all!" was the dream.

At last it was over, the votes cast and counted. And the count showed that a million Americans had voted for Eugene Debs.

Under the circumstances, the size of the socialist vote was amazing. But what exactly did that million votes mean? Debs tried to interpret.

Without persuasive speeches, without bands and marches and the magic of the candidate in person—on a flag-draped stage, on the rear platform of a train, on the hood of a Ford—a million Americans had voted for a sixty-five-year-old inmate of the federal prison in Atlanta. From any point of view, it was assuredly gratifying. Though the Socialist party had polled only a few more votes than in 1912, a million was nevertheless an impressive number.

Of course, certain facts had to be taken into consideration.

1920 Campaign Buttons
Convict #9653 polled close to one million votes.

Walls and Bars

Debs reminded himself that women could now vote as well as men. Many socialists, moreover, had gone over to the Communist party. Little as he wanted to believe it, it was nevertheless obvious to Debs that the Socialist party was dying. Probably many of the votes cast for him had been simply protest votes.

Protest against what? The System?

Even before the vote was counted, Debs said that he hoped for everything and expected nothing. But now as he analyzed the results of the election he was deeply troubled. Did the protest have direction? Or was it blind? Was it *against* what was but not *for* what could be?

It saddened Eugene to think that after all his efforts to draw a picture of the beautiful world socialism could create, the American people did not see that beautiful world. He was troubled that Americans didn't seem to want anything. And they could have everything they wanted.

19

Good-bye to Atlanta

Would Eugene Debs be pardoned?

As long as Woodrow Wilson was president, there wasn't the least chance of it. His own attorney general, A. Mitchell Palmer, had urged that Eugene Debs was in poor health, that he was sixty-five years old, and that his friends were afraid he might die in prison. The president had lost his temper.

"I will never consent to the pardon of this man!" he stormed when the recommendation for pardon came across his desk. "While the flower of American youth was pouring out its blood, this man, Debs, stood behind the line, snipping, attacking, and denouncing them. This man was a traitor to his country, and he will never be pardoned during my administration." Across the recommendation he wrote one word: DENIED.

When Debs heard about the matter, he was upset. It looked as if he had asked for a pardon. He told a visisting reporter how he felt about it, and next day the *New York Times* carried the following statement:

"I understand perfectly the feelings of Wilson when he reviews what he has done. When he realizes the suffering he has brought about, then he is being punished. It is he, not I, who needs a pardon. . . . Woodrow Wilson is an exile from the hearts of his people. The betrayal of his ideals makes him the most pathetic figure in the world."

That statement cost Eugene his visiting and writing privileges for an indefinite period. Wilson saw to that.

In 1921 a new president came into the White House. Warren G. Harding let it be known from the first that he was in favor of pardoning political prisoners. It wasn't long before he asked his attorney general, Harry M. Daugherty, to look into the Debs case, and Eugene was sent for. He went to Washington alone and unguarded. Mr. Daugherty's report was most favorable. Indeed, he thought he had never met a man he liked better. Had it not been for the protests of the American Legion, Debs would have been released on the Fourth of July.

"Be patient, Gene. Just hang on till Christmas," his friends said. Everyone who visited him brought hopeful news.

Among those who came to see Debs at this time was one with whom he did not discuss amnesty and toward whom he had been hostile every since the Pullman strike—Samuel Gompers. The chief of the AFL was in Atlanta for the national convention of his organization. The warden invited him to address the prisoners, and afterward he met Debs in the warden's office. Gompers looked prosperous in his well-tailored suit. Eugene was wearing his usual prison blue, with sneakers on his feet over coarse socks.

"How do you do, Mr. Gompers," Debs said stiffly.

"How do you do, Gene," Gompers replied. He was taken aback by Debs's formal manner. "Many years ago," Gompers said, "you called me Sam. Can't we get back on those terms again?"

Debs remembered how Gompers had failed to support the Pullman strike and how he had refused to carry to the General Managers his offer to end the strike provided the strikers were rehired. Debs remembered how Gompers had not raised his voice when Haywood and Moyer were charged with murder. In his well-dressed visitor Eugene saw a betrayer of the working class, a misleader who hobnobbed with millionaires and opposed industrial unions. Eugene despised the man he had once looked up to.

"Perhaps some day we can," he answered coldly.

After exchanging a few commonplaces, Eugene went back to his work in the hospital.

On December 23, 1921, the White House made a long awaited announcement: Eugene Debs and twenty-three other political prisoners would be released on Christmas Day. For Eugene there was a special word: the president invited him to come to the White House.

Debs didn't hear the good news till the day before Christmas. His first reaction was pain: he would leave behind the many prisoners who had come to trust and depend on him. Then came overwhelming joy. Home! . . . home and Kate! He had not seen

127

his wife since he left Terre Haute and thrown her a last good-bye kiss from the train. Doubtless for reasons of their own, it had been agreed between them that Kate would not come to Atlanta. But she had written lovingly and faithfully.

His third Christmas in prison! He had entered Moundsville April 13, 1919. Tomorrow would be December 25, 1921. He had been in prison a little over two years and eight months. It seemed long. But some of the prisoners would be staying in Atlanta all their lives!

The next day he sent Kate a wire. He was coming home to her, his beloved. The day of their blessed communion was near. But he had to make a necessary trip to Washington first. With an overflowing heart he embraced and blessed her.

It was afternoon when Eugene left the prison.

Together with the warden and deputy warden he walked out toward the gate, where a car was waiting. They were halfway across the open space between the prison and the gate when a thunderous sound burst from the cell blocks behind them. They wheeled about in astonishment. Eugene's heart almost stopped beating as he saw hundreds of prisoners pressing their tearful faces against the barred prison windows. The impulse seized him to turn back. He felt that he had no right to leave. Tears that he could not stop, nor wanted to, streamed down his face.

He lifted his hat and held it motionless above his head. It was his farewell to the insulted and injured he was leaving behind.

But he had to go. As he stepped into the waiting car and waved his hat for the last time, another mighty shout burst out, then another and another.

Good-bye to Atlanta

Far up on the winding road the last faint echo of the convict cheering died away.

An invitation to call at the White House is a command.

"Good-morning, Mr. President," Eugene said to the handsome man seated behind a desk in the president's office.

Warren G. Harding, fresh, full of life, smiling, went forward to meet Eugene. They shook hands—the President and the prisoner who had run for President.

"Well, I have heard so damned much about you, Mr. Debs," Harding said cordially, "that I am now very glad to meet you personally."

He led Eugene to a chair and they talked—about Atlanta and prisoners and prisons. . . .

When Eugene came out, he was bombarded with questions from a throng of reporters, for he was the greatest public figure in America.

"How did you like the president?" "How do you like the White House?"

Eugene's eyes lit up. This was so like old times!

"Mr. Harding appears to me to be a kind gentleman," he said. And drawing a breath, he added, "One who I believe possesses humane impulses. We understood each other perfectly. As for the White House"—he broke into a grin—"well, gentlemen, my personal perference is to live privately as an humble citizen in my cottage at Terre Haute."

The news was already out that Eugene Debs was in Washington at the president's invitation. That day all sorts of people came

129

to Eugene's hotel room to wish him well. Many were distinguished men. But Debs was no publicity seeker, had never been one, and all he wanted now was to get home.

Meantime in Terre Haute three different groups had been working to make Eugene's homecoming sensational. Eugene had wired that his train would arrive at 3:40 in the afternoon on the twenty-eighth. This news threw the reception committee into a panic. Workingmen from all Indiana intended to be on hand to meet the train. How could coal miners and factory workers be expected to leave their jobs in order to get to Terre Haute in time? Eugene was arriving at an inconvenient hour!

Charles Ervin, editor of the *New York Call* (the socialist daily), hastily wired Eugene not to arrive till eight o'clock. He must stay over in Indianapolis for four hours. To make sure that nothing went wrong, someone was sent off to meet him in Indianapolis.

The moment came. While Kate waited for Eugene at the front door of their home, thirty thousand excited, joyous people milled around at the railway station. Each sported a little white card tied on with red ribbon and saying: "Welcome home—Gene Debs." Every fire bell in Terre Haute was ringing, every church bell was chiming when the train pulled in.

Eugene stepped down from the coach. Strong hands hoisted him on shoulders high above the crowd and he was carried to a wagon drawn up near the station. It was the very wagon he had ridden in the day he came home from Woodstock!

Dozens of hands grasped the ropes to draw Eugene home while the crowd fell in behind and on either side. A Negro band played "Swing Low, Sweet Chariot."

20

"The Inevitable Cannot Die"

Eugene was home. The dream that had enabled him to endure the harsh life in prison had come true. And his first reaction was to collapse. Ailments that he had denied because he refused to die in jail asserted themselves. He had to come to terms with the fact that prison food had ruined his stomach and kidneys, that headaches and lumbago and rheumatism were a daily torment, that his heart was playing tricks.

He was tired, tired. But people didn't, or wouldn't, understand that he had to be left in peace. Every minute the phone rang. Mail was dropped at the front door in sacks. Telegrams and special delivery letters came, asking him to lecture, write articles, make statements. There were even four invitations to appear in vaudeville. One person offered him $2,000 if he would just walk across the stage.

At night he could not sleep. Lying awake in his comfortable bed, he was again behind prison walls. The forms and faces of the spiritless men he had known surrounded him. He heard their voices: "Mr. Debs, I want to get a minute with you to tell you about my case." "Mr. Debs, will you read this letter from my wife? She says she can't stand the gaff any longer." "Mr. Debs! Mr. Debs! Mr. Debs!" All he had been able to do was listen and comfort and advise. How many "bad" prisoners had brought him their letters soaked in tears!

One face in particular haunted him. It was the face of a man who had spent nearly forty-eight of his fifty-five years in reformatories and prisons. At the age of seven he had been sent to a house of correction, where he had been starved and beaten and had learned to steal. He had run away, only to dodge detectives who were forever on his track. They said he was "bad." They were determined that he should be kept out of sight, behind prison walls.

"Doomed in his cradle," Eugene said to himself. "Doomed by the system."

What could he do for this prisoner, for the twenty-three hundred prisoners he had left behind at Atlanta?

He had to tell their story. . . .

Though it was the middle of the night, Eugene forced himself to get out of bed. He found paper and pencil and made himself sit down at his rolltop desk. How often had he sat thus writing and writing half the night for the BLF! How often had he fallen asleep at his desk and his mother's hand had put out the light! A lifetime

"The Inevitable Cannot Die"

had passed since then. Now he had other things to say. He had to tell America what prisons were. He must explain their meaning.

"You are committing suicide," his doctor solemnly warned Eugene.

He paid no attention. He had been asked by the Bell Syndicate to write twelve articles about Atlanta. They would be published in newspapers throughout the country. He needed the money, but his need to do something for the prisoners hounded him more.

If only his health were what it had been when he was defending Moyer and Haywood! Eugene soon realized that he could not get through the exhausting work alone. He thought of the young reporter who had gone to the doors of Moundsville with him and had come a dozen or more times to see him in prison. David Karsner was now an editor of the *New York Call*. He was like a younger spiritual brother to him.

In the middle of March 1922, Karsner came to Terre Haute to take the prison story from Eugene's heart. Every morning Debs dictated his memories of the prisons he had known. The memories were so vivid, so tearing, they dealt so much with cruelty, with indifference, and despair that sometimes after an hour Eugene could work no more. He knew that he must restrain himself. Unless he toned down his writing, the articles would never be published. Yet try as he would, the sentences came out shocking and bitter.

At last the first of the articles appeared. A heading said in part: "Mr. Debs has agreed not to insert any political propaganda into the articles."

He had agreed to no such thing. He had reserved the right to show that poverty had its roots in capitalism. What was the sense of writing about prisons if he didn't point out that the capitalist system breeds poverty and that proverty breeds crime?

He protested. The editors were unyielding. Newspapers were ready enough to publish the horrors of prison life, the more horror the better. But they didn't want any unpleasant comments about the capitalist system.

Debs's first nine articles were heavily cut. His last three were not published at all.

But the prison articles were not the only thing that worried Debs. He was constantly being asked to declare where he stood politically. Members of the Communist party came to see him. Members of the Socialist party came to see him.

"I am a socialist!" Debs declared. That should be enough! Why must he declare for one party or another?

All the same he did what he had always done. He remained a member of the Socialist party. He wouldn't go to its meetings nor accept any speaking engagements for it. He disapproved of what was going on inside. Instead of promoting industrial unions, the Party was going along with Gompers and his AFL. Where was the class struggle? It had disappeared from the Party's thinking. The Party was a reform party trying to get its members elected to office.

Physically Debs was slowly losing ground. He couldn't walk a dozen blocks without being exhausted. In the summer of 1922 he decided to go to a nature-cure sanitarium not far from Chicago. Two or three months of rest, he thought, and a diet of grain and fresh fruit were what he needed to be himself again.

But changing the scene and the diet did not do the trick. He could not stem his pace. People insisted on coming to talk with

134

Debs with poet Carl Sandburg

him. Letters kept coming. Newspapers published articles about him that upset Eugene.

Perhaps what hurt him most—though he wouldn't admit it—was that the Brotherhood of Locomotive Firemen rejected him. At least, that's what he thought. At their convention they voted down a proposal that Eugene Debs be invited to speak. He wrote a long release to the papers about that. He said that he didn't start out expecting gratitude and wasn't disappointed. At the end he said: "My heart has been, is, and always will be with the working class, and even though they deny me and reject me and turn me from their ranks, they can never turn themselves from my heart."

Late that fall Eugene Debs went back to Terre Haute. He thought he was well, but by Christmas he was again in bed. He would have to spend most of the next five years taking care of his health.

Kate, whose mother was now dead, was herself unwell. Nevertheless she looked after Eugene as devotedly as she had always done, while Theodore stood by. . . .

And in the end? Was Eugene true to his vision to the very end?

He did not change. He had "hitched his wagon to a star" and it was not the kind that shoots through the sky on an August night.

"Socialism must follow capitalism as the dawn follows night," he said. And again: "Socialism will never die. It is inevitable. The inevitable cannot die."

At times, when he recovered from a bout with illness, Eugene would go on a lecture tour; people still flocked to hear him. But his greatest satisfaction came when in January 1926 he began to edit a labor paper, the *American Appeal*. Sitting at his editorial desk,

135

Debs was a happy man. He was back again where he started—fighting for justice. In his first number he pleaded for the lives of Sacco and Vanzetti, two immigrant Italian anarchists who were to be executed for a murder they had not committed.

The *American Appeal* was just the right name for his paper because its editor was so completely an American. Eugene had never been abroad. Nor had he any desire to be anywhere but in America. When he did go, it was only to Bermuda and only for the sake of his wife, who was very unwell. He returned without regret. "Bermuda is a fine place," he said. "But I'm glad to be back in America."

From then on, Eugene thought a good deal about death. But he didn't guess it was so near. Nor did he have a notion of the widespread grief his death would cause. He had always thought that Eugene Debs the man was unimportant, and that only his faith in a better society mattered. But the two could not be separated: the man and the idea were one.

All America grieved when newspapers reported that on October 20, 1926, Eugene Debs had died.

From coast to coast memorial meetings were held. In Chicago eight thousand met to pay him tribute. In New York uncounted thousands marched in the rain. In Terre Haute, where his body lay in state for two days at the Labor Temple, workers of a dozen different trades told one another how, years ago, Gene had helped them organize their union.

People came from hundreds of miles away to say a last goodbye. Some came because they were Eugene's personal friends and loved him. Among them were famous writers, poets, noted lawyers, successful business men. But many more who

136

"The Inevitable Cannot Die"

came were ordinary workers who dug coal, worked on trains, operated machines, labored on farms. They, too, loved Eugene. They said that he belonged to them.

Dressed in their Sunday best, they filed thoughtfully past the coffin. Nothing would ever take Eugene Debs from their hearts. He had fought their fight. He had given them his dream. Eugene Debs—they would never see his like again.